D1211957

CHINA

Xinghua Jun •

Puyang Path

Quanzhou •

Liuwu Dian
Xiamen •
Zhangzhou •   Jinmen
Gulang Yu

Tropicus   Cancri

Yu Yonghe's
Tales of
Formosa

郁永河的裨海紀遊

25

24

23

22

135   130

Out of China

OR

YU YONGHE'S TALE OF FORMOSA

.

A HISTORY OF SEVENTEENTH-CENTURY TAIWAN

Macabe Keliher

SMC Publishing Inc. | Taipei

SMC PUBLISHING INC.

P.O. Box 13–342, Taipei 106, Taiwan

Tel: (886-2)2362-0190 Fax: (886-2)2362-3834

email: weitw@smcbook.com.tw

http://www.smcbook.com.tw

COPYRIGHT © 2003 BY MACABE KELIHER

All rights reserved. No part of this publication may be re-produced,
stored in a retrieval system, or transmitted, in any form or by any
means, electronic, mechanical, photocopying, recording or otherwise,
without the author's permission.

ISBN 957-638-608-x (cloth)
ISBN 957-638-609-8 (paper)

Designed by Alicia Beebe

Set in Goudy
Chapter titles in Carmilla
Printed on acid-free paper

Printed in Taiwan

for shengfang

in search of her past...and her future

Guantang Island
(Mazu)

ou

зkou

Danshui

Yu's Camp

Heping Island

Jilong

Formosa

Nankan

Zhuqian (Hsinchu)

Houlong

Wanli

Shalu

Penghu

Bianxian

Da-wu-jun

Caili

Zhuluo

Da-wu-jun

Ou
Wang

Madou

Jia-li-xing

Lu-er-men

Xingang

Taiwan Fu (Tainan)

Fengshan
(Kaohsiung)

TAÏ-OUAN ou ISLE FORMOSE

Latitude Septentrionale.
Noorder breedte.

25

24

23

22

37

138

139

140

Out of China

I have traveled to distant shores,
and to far away lands where men do not venture.
I have been to the heights of the mountains
and the depths of the rivers,
I have escaped death
from the island's most cunning dangers.
I have lived the lives of the savages,
I have walked through it all;
how can I not leave word to let the rest of the world know.

YU YONGHE

Contents

Chronology

NOTE ON CHINESE SPELLINGS

After much agonizing and incessant prodding from colleagues, I have opted to use the pinyin system of romanization. It is not an ideal choice for romanizing Chinese words, however it is the most widely used and most commonly accepted. The pinyin system's exceptions to pronouncing words like they look are more than a few (most unreasonably for the creators' willingness to please their Russian advisors by partially adopting forms similar to the Cyrillic Alphabet.) Thus the pinyin "q" stands for the sound which is more readily suggested by "ch". Elsewhere, the pinyin "c" should be pronounced like "ts", the "x" like "sh" or "sy", and "zh" as a hard "j". For Chinese speakers, a character list can be found on page 227.

AUTHOR'S NOTE

T he diaries on which *Out of China* is based frame an era which defined Taiwan. In the seventeenth century the island underwent developments that set the direction for all that would follow, including the conflicts it would face for the next three hundred years up to the present day.

For Taiwan, the seventeenth century stands as one of those periods in history in which a country is born and comes to maturity, a pivotal era in which emperors fall and nothing is ever again the same. For Europe, one might point to the first thirty years of the ninteenth century; for the US, the hundred years between its founding to the end of the civil war; and for Japan, to the Meiji Restoration.

Before the seventeenth century, Chinese considered Taiwan to be, as Qing emperor Kangxi later called it, "a mud ball in the sea." Fishermen might have visited its waters, or imperial excursions sailed by, but it remained as indistinct as any other remote island. Only seven or eight hundred Chinese had come to reside there by the early seventeenth century, and mostly migratory fisherman. It had not even its own name; being called "Little Liuqiu", or the "Eastern Savage Land", or something else of comparable nature.

The arrival of the Dutch in the 1620s changed all that. For one thing, they made the name of Formosa widespread among Europeans, and instituted the pronunciation of "Taiwan" to refer to the harbor at Tainan. From this harbor the Dutch turned Taiwan into a profitable trading base and built an export market—the beginnings of what would come to define the island's economy. The Dutch also undertook a massive pacification effort which subdued most of the wild and headhunting aborigines, making the land safe for immigrating Chinese. From the few hundred Chinese that managed to survive aborigine raids before the Dutch colonial government, as many as one hundred thousand could prosper by the time the Europeans were pushed out by Zheng Chenggong (Koxinga) in 1662.

While the Dutch laid the foundations of an economic and administrative infrastructure, the Zhengs reinforced it with Sinicization. Assuming the role of rulers when the defeated Dutch were forced out, the Zheng government went about instituting Chinese education, exams, chopsticks, temples and Chinese rituals. This set the stage for continued tension with China. Although the Zheng ruler, Zheng Jing, called himself the King of Taiwan, and claimed his independence in a manner like Japan and the Philippines, the Qing refused on the grounds that "you are Chinese and not foreign barbarians."

That tension turned to war in 1683 when the Qing invaded, using tactics that the People's Liberation Army still studies today. Through an approach of economic pressures and "refusing to relinquish the use of force", the Qing carried off a successful attack and retired the Zheng government. They subsequently occupied the island for the next two hundred years.

This was the Taiwan this book's main character Yu Yonghe visited in 1697. He talked with participants of the events just past and took notes on the lingering effects of previous rulers. Given the tumultuous experiences the island had gone through in the past century, as well as the sea crossing, it is no surprise that China knew very little if anything at all about the island. Yu's main purpose in publishing his diaries when he returned was to inform the Chinese speaking world of Taiwan.

My purpose in revisiting these diaries is to re-invoke the seventeenth century, a period of Taiwan history where research is just beginning, and hardly anything has been published in English. Although *Out of China* remains faithful to Yu's story as he travels from Fuzhou, China to Taiwan and back again, I have interjected the narrative with sketches of the characters and trends of the time. It is far from exhaustive, but is meant, rather, as a glimpse of an era long past, seen through the eyes of a contemporary and supplemented with just enough of what he didn't see to understand what still haunts us today.

This book has been rushed to print in early 2003 in occasion for a major exhibition at the Taipei National Palace Museum: The Emergence of Taiwan on the World Scene in the 17th Century. *If readers have any comments or corrections I would be grateful if they would write to me at my private address: Box 1-457, Mucha Taipei 116; or email: mac@macabe.net; and if they find any expressions or opinions of mine insupportable, they are welcome to give me their comments so that I may weigh them. Also, those interested in the diary itself will be happy to know that I am currently working on a complete translation.*

mk
Mucha, Taipei
February 2003

PREFACE

BY TU CHENG-SHENG, DIRECTOR OF THE NATIONAL PALACE MUSEUM

The character in *Out of China*, Yu Yonghe, was a unique man, as far as Chinese literati are concerned, which makes his work, *Pihai Jiyou*, or *The Small Sea Travel Records*, just as unique and similarly interesting. Macabe Keliher's translation of Yu's text gives us a better understanding of Taiwan's early history, and I am very pleased to have been one of the first to read it and to recommend it for all to pick up.

We know very little about Yu Yonghe, only that he was from Zhejiang province, Renhe prefecture (near Hangzhou). Scholars of the Qing dynasty could not find any further information on him, and academics today have little to add. But from the single work that the man left behind we can deduce much. He was born before 1650 and was very familiar with the Chinese classics. His poetry was not bad even if he never sat for imperial examinations or became an official. Yu liked to travel. Although he had a mother at home, he did not rule out traveling to far away places. He went to every corner of Fujian and even to the place considered to be the most desolate and barbaric: Taiwan. We don't know his profession but he was familiar with many provincial and county officials, which suggests that he had some financial means, possibly as a land owner or member of the gentry class.

Unlike other intellectuals and literati of the day, Yu had some knowledge of foreigners and was extremely interested in overseas lands. His writings on the Zhengs (偽鄭逸事), the aborigines (番境補遺), and China's south-eastern seas (海上紀略 and 宇內形勢), stand as proof of this. Chinese literati rarely traveled abroad unless they were sent on official assignment or had the misfortune to be exiled. Of course they all went to the scenic spots of historical interest, such as the Five Sacred Mountains, but one is hard pressed to find a character like Yu Yonghe who visited overseas lands and left such a vivid account. It is against this historical context that Yu is unique.

Yu was, however, constrained by the traditions and culture of the time. His knowledge of Japan, the Red Hair Barbarians and other Western countries was full of hearsay and cannot be compared to the knowledge that Western explorers had of East Asia at the time. But this was China's failing and not just Yu's. The burden of responsibility and blame cannot be placed entirely on his shoulders.

The backdrop of Yu's journey to Taiwan was the explosion of the Fuzhou gunpowder stores in 1696. Early the next year Fujian officials sent Yu to Taiwan to mine sulfur. Yu traveled down the China coast to Xiamen and crossed the Taiwan Strait, stopping over in Penghu before landing in Tai-nan. Following the western coast of the island, Yu traveled northward to Danshui and Beitou where he bought amorphous sulfur from local aborigines and melted it down to make pure sulfur.

In the winter of that same year he returned to Fuzhou. Over the course of his 10-month journey he kept a diary of all that he saw and heard. It became *The Small Sea Travel Records*. Because Yu's mission was to collect sulfur, his book is sometimes referred to as the *Sulfur Extraction Diaries*. With either name, it is an account of an author's personal experiences and one of the most vivid historical records of the period. From very early on it became the most talked about travelogue and was incorporated into many libraries and collections.

When Yu arrived to Taiwan, the Qing had already administered the island for thirteen years. The Dutch had arrived seventy-three years earlier, and Zheng Chenggong (Koxinga) had driven them out only thirty-five years before Yu. With these events just past, Yu not only recorded the developments of the era, but he also observed what the Dutch and the Zhengs left behind, including administrative structures. He heard the tales of witnesses to events just past and observed an aborigine culture still relatively untouched. Yu's recordings offer an abundance of first hand information. In fact, these diaries reflect the multicultural characteristics of early Taiwan.

Other primary records of the seventeenth century are limited to those of conquerors and administrators. The Dutch records are in this hand, as are those of the Qing. The Zhengs left very little behind in the way of records.

Although Yu traveled to Taiwan on assignment, he was not an official, and his book is the observation of a compassionate literati rather than a government report. Yu expresses the injustice done to the aborigines, even if he cannot escape the prejudices of his time and identify with the aborigines and their culture. Yet this problem of how to study the aborigines so called "uncivilized" ways is something contemporary scholars are still grappling with today, and we cannot place too high an expectation on Yu.

Yu's diaries have a sort of eclectic discussion of events past, and although Keliher follows Yu's narrative and historical commentary, *Out of China* is not a simple translation. Keliher uses Yu's diaries as a base to construct a history of Taiwan in the seventeenth century. Here we can read of Zheng Chenggong, Shi Lang, the Qing Dynasty and Taiwan's historical developments, as well as the Dutch and the Spanish, of which Yu knew very little. Although *The Small Sea Travel Records* is fascinating for the adventure tale alone, it is easy to overstate the dangers of the island. After years of Dutch, Spanish and Zheng repression and exploitation, Taiwan was not exactly a hostile hell. The feeling Yu gives of a horrible and savage land is perhaps a bit overdone. Keliher has been able to compensate by drawing on other source materials, making the record more historical and less fictitious.

The text of the original diary is not easy to wade through nor understand, but Keliher's translation and treatment of it is quite suitable. He has handled its subtlety and preserved its meaning. His reorganization and value-added history has created a unique picture of seventeenth-century Taiwan. His historical insights and exploration of other source materials draws out the content of Yu's narrative, making *Out of China* a must read for Taiwanese wanting to know of their own history, or for foreigners hoping to understand it.

Tu Cheng-sheng
Director of the National Palace Museum
Member of Academia Sinica
February 20, 2003

Out of China

I was born and I will die. The Creator will decide, so what can water and earth do to me!

YU YONGHE

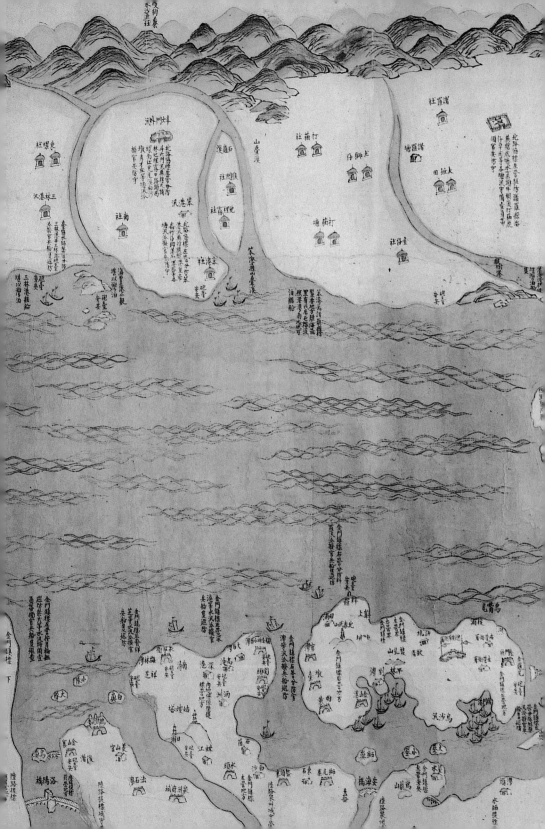

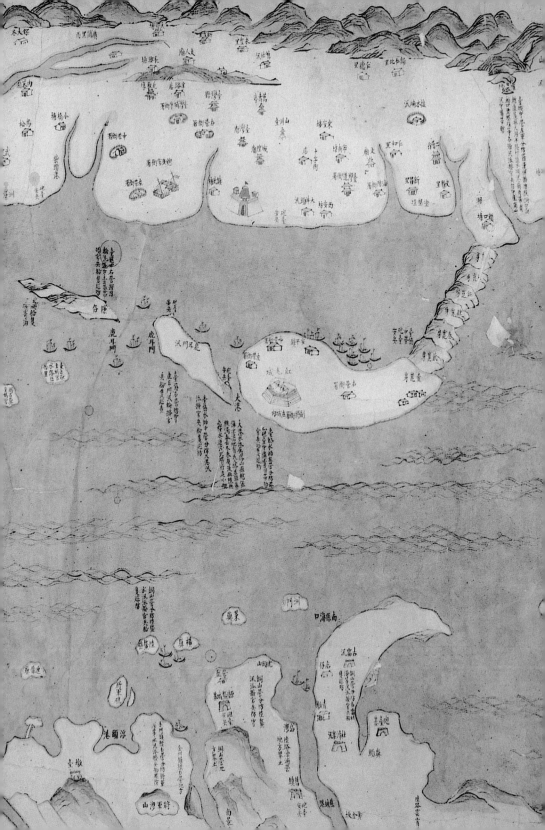

Prologue

The imperial gunpowder stores have exploded. When the ensuing fire stops burning, not a trace of the sulfur-nitrate remains. More than five hundred thousand pounds of it has gone up in flames, the dry earth consuming it all, leaving behind not even ash.

It is Fuzhou, China. It is the winter of 1696.

A drought has already afflicted five of Fujian province's eight counties, including the capital, Fuzhou. Just months before the gunpowder store fire, officials duly noted, "tax revenues will be down this year."[1] Now they have another problem: how to replace the lost gunpowder? Local officials must take full responsibility, and the cost to replenish the stores must come from their own purse.

The officials have heard that the recently occupied island of Taiwan, just 150 km off the coast of Fujian, has rich sulfur stores. More than half a century ago, a young subject of the previous dynasty wrote a short work on "How to Extract Sulfur from the Taiwan Dirt."[2] He obtained his expertise from aborigines who were selling sulfur to Chinese pirates in amounts of up to five hundred thousand pounds a year. The natives in the area had long mined the mineral and traded it to other tribes for use in primitive fireworks.

With such a large trade, the Spanish were keen to get into the market, and made the northern sulfur stores one of their prime arguments for building a fort on the island. As early as 1632, Fr. Jacinto Esquivel noted in a letter to the Spanish King that "sulfur is abundant along the Tamsui (Danshui) River, in the village of Quipatao (Beitou)."[3] Some ten years later, thanks to the Spanish incentive, a vibrant sulfur trade flourished between the colonizers and the aborigines. The Dutch, eager to get into the trade, drove out the Spanish in the 1640s and took to mining the mineral in quantities of one-hundred thousand pounds a year.[4]

By 1696, both the Spanish and Dutch have long retired from the island —in part due to the sulfur trade's lack of profits—and although the Qing Dynasty officially added Taiwan to its map in 1684, neither the central, nor any of the local governments, have attempted to exploit the rich sulfur resources. Now the Fuzhou gunpowder store explosion has caused an immediate need and both governments are curious to see if the new Taiwan territory, far off at sea, has any potential to replenish imperial stores.

Fuzhou officials plan to organize a party to travel to the north of Taiwan, to mine the mineral and bring it back to use in the manufacturing of gunpowder. They have another problem, though, who will lead the party? There are few volunteers to make a trip across a strait that sucks many who try to a salty death at the bottom of the sea. Or to venture through territory home to aborigines known for their headhunting practices. And few want to live for months on end, perhaps even years, in a wild place devoid of people while they extract sulfur everyday. Furthermore, there will be little reward for someone who does. No official rank, no promotion, no audience with the emperor. The Fuzhou officials might as well give up their plan.

Yu Yonghe is already in Fujian. He has traveled from his home in neighboring Zhejiang province to explore the mountains and rivers. Yu thrives on adventure and wallows in danger. He climbs mountains of towering cliffs and floats down rivers in bamboo rafts. He wants to go everywhere and to see everything. He wants to climb every peak and explore every forest. In this regard, Yu is a unique official, if he is an official at all. Yu never says as much, nor refers to himself as a holder of rank—nor does anyone else in discussing him throughout history. But his close relations with the provincial government, his writings and his frequent poems indicate that he is a man of some stature; perhaps a well-to-do literati, spending his days composing verse and mountain climbing. Yet even for this social class, Yu's activities are extraordinary. Scholars of the day were most wont to spend their time in study, memorization and learning, and officials were often bogged down by managing their administrative affairs. Neither took to travel and exploration, and only high officials would tour neighboring provinces.

Yet by the fall of 1696, Yu has been through six of Fujian's eight counties. Traveling on his own, he has seen the coast and ventured through Zhangzhou and Quanzhou, the two port cities closest to Taiwan. It is here that Yu hears the first tales of the island at sea just over the horizon. Around 80 percent of the Chinese immigrating to Taiwan come from one of these two cities. About 45 percent of the population in Taiwan comes from Quanzhou, and 35 percent from Zhangzhou. Early bans on travel as a direct result of the imperial navy admiral's prejudice against Guangdong residents kept numbers from the port city Chaozhou relatively low, at around 16 percent. By the twentieth century these figures have played themselves out to a definite conclusion, whereby in 1926, of 3.75 million Taiwanese, 3.1 million will be able to trace their roots back to Fujian and only 580,000 to Guangdong.[5]

The merchants and farmers that Yu meets in Zhangzhou and Quanzhou have traveled to Taiwan and seen its shores. They have touched the rugged wilderness and gazed up at the peaks that tower three thousand meters into the clouds. They have fought with the aborigines and seen their brothers' heads carried off by them. The tales excite Yu who responds to their warnings with, "I like adventure; I will not avoid danger."[6] As he completes his tour of Fujian, bringing the last two counties into his travel repertoire, he remarks, "I have been through all of Fujian's eight prefectures. Now Taiwan has become the ninth but I still do not know what it looks like."[7]

His yearning is innocent and apolitical, but Taiwan has already caused countless headaches for China's rulers. It had only come under Qing rule recently. As the Manchus swept the Chinese countryside in the mid-seventeenth century, the last of the remaining Ming Dynasty defenders, under the command of Zheng Chenggong (better known to the west as Koxinga), fled to the island in 1661 and set up a Chinese colony. As the Chinese population on Taiwan doubled to over 100,000, the Qing Dynasty, under continuous coastal threat and fearing future challenges to its sovereignty, fought a stalemated war for over two decades against the Zheng family. In 1683, the Zheng forces had exhausted themselves and capitulated. Emperor Kangxi, at the urging of his naval commander in chief, opted to send civilian officials and a military garrison to Taiwan, "bringing it into our territory."[8]

Yet even after the imperial edict was sent out across China, few knew of the island. The only work written on Taiwan for the Chinese speaking world was at the turn of the sixteenth century. A Chinese literati, Chen Di, accompanied the Ming Navy on a punitive expedition that took them to Taiwan in search of pirates. Upon their return, Chen composed a slim pamphlet entitled *Records of the Eastern Savages* in which he offered some of the first records of the island and the aborigine tribes.[9] Since then, the Dutch, the Spanish and the Zheng Family have all presided over Taiwan, but those in China knew little about their regimes, if anything at all. They knew even less about the island's geography, the diversity of the aborigine tribes, or even the Chinese immigrants who have recently settled there. Yu says he wants to travel to Taiwan not just for the adventure but to bring back word about the island. He proposes to keep a diary of his experiences and observations so that "the rest of the world will know."

His friends say that is grand, but they also know the island is not at peace under Qing rule. From the time the Qing established administrative structures on the island, settler backlash against oppressive officials and heavy taxes have rocked the frontier. In 1684, the first year the dynasty brought Taiwan under their control, two major uprisings exploded against the new government. The Qing showed no mercy to the rebels, killing over one thousand of them in the second rebellion alone. But many escaped and hid in the mountains, never to be caught.[10]

Yu's family and friends plead with him not to go.

A great distance stands between Fujian and Taiwan, alienating the previous generations from any contact. Although early references describe many barbarian islands in detail, none of them mention Taiwan.

YU YONGHE

國初沿海設兵大牙相制為衛者四萬所者十謂之正兵以控禦於
中為寨者五萬墩舖等費西數謂之遊兵以哨守於外而又有黃
崎等二鎮兵洪洪等四十二巡司弓兵安遶等八捕溢民壯其為
之備守為文應地廣官課難於責成隨地設官大小相維有副使
一貝巡視於上謂之海有都撰

塞有把總指揮各臺有
地撿等官文萬之分理為平屈則信地以守墩報則合力以攻一
號召之間而兵船數百可以立齊一勤一捕之徵而兵夫數千可以

走出中國

小琉球國

北山

PART 1

Out of China

Dutch engraving of Xiamen (Amoy), first published in 1667.

Chinese map of the Fujian coast and islands, from the late sixteenth century.
The island at center top, "Xiao Liuqiu Guo," is Taiwan.

Out of China

Yu Yonghe has won the honor of leading the expedition party to Taiwan. Few, however, would call it an honor given the great dangers — the strait crossing, the hostile aborigines, the diseases, possibly even death. It is not an assignment that brings great esteem, nor will it lead to promotion. In fact, no one else has volunteered and Fuzhou city authorities are happy to find someone eager for the job. Yu must travel south, down the coast of China to Xiamen, where he will have to hire a captain to take him across the Taiwan strait to the county seat at Taiwan Fu.**

If he makes it safely across the strait, he must find laborers and buy supplies

---

* First month, twenty-fourth day, thirty-sixth year of the Kangxi reign. Yu uses dates corresponding to the lunar calendar and the year of emperor's reign. I have translated these into Gregorian calendar dates.

** Taiwan Fu 臺灣府 was the name of Tainan 臺南 from 1684 to the mid 1800s.

for a journey of over three hundred kilometers to the north of the island where he must mine sulfur in an unsettled and unforgiving environment.

To the average official it may sound like a punishment, perhaps even banishment, but not to Yu. Yu is adventurous, energetic and rambunctious. He delights in exploring new lands and meeting new peoples. He has scaled all of the peaks in Fujian and rafted down most of the province's rivers. Once, when confronted by a friend for what he considered reckless acts, Yu told him that he always chooses the more daring rout over the safe and unexciting one. "I was born and I will die," Yu said, "The Creator will decide, so what can water and earth do to me!" Taiwan is not a punishment for Yu. Not at all. Taiwan is a calling.[1]

It is the twenty-fourth day of the first month in the thirty-sixth year of the Kangxi Reign.

Yu is eager to begin the journey. His friend Wang Yunsen will accompany him, as will Yu's three servants who will assist him in his personal needs during the journey. At noon, just after lunch, they set off, crossing Fuzhou's Nantai Bridge out of the city. A friend, Cao Luyang, accompanies them, and it is a good thing for soon torrential rains force them to take cover. They retire to Cao's house where they stay for the night hoping the rain will ease up the next day.

FEBRUARY 16

FUZHOU

The skies have cleared. Yu and his party set out early in the morning, walking at a brisk pace. At kilometer fifteen they cross the Wulong River. Yu notes the water's silky smooth glow, so still that it creates a perfect reflection of the lighthouse standing at the water's edge.

As evening falls they reach Fangkou, some 60 kilometers southeast Fuzhou. The town is small and word spreads quickly that travelers on their way to Taiwan have arrived for the night. A young Dong Zanhou and his nephew come to drink tea with Yu and Wang. Dong is the oldest son of the magistrate of Taiwan's Zhulo* County. Learning that the party has been sent by the Fujian government and will certainly have safe transportation across the strait, Dong decides this is a good opportunity to travel to Zhuluo and see his father.

Both Dong and his nephew will accompany Yu.

FEBRUARY 17
LOVESICK PEAK

Yu is perhaps 50 years old. He feels age catching up to him as they cross Lovesick Peak, a hill that he has been over six times. This time it takes Yu more effort to cross than in the past. "I am getting old,"he writes, "my teeth and hair are falling out, life has already surpassed me."

That night they stay in Yuxi.

FEBRUARY 18
XINGHUA JUN

Yu and his party set out in the early morning before the sun has burned the mist off the fields. The farmers have also risen early. They walk up and down the rows of grain behind a plow pulled by oxen. The scene touches Yu who composes a poem:

The color of the mountains,
  the rivers clear and flowing.
I hear the sound of people
  and a far off dog barking.
The mist leaves one wet
  and the cold makes one shiver.
The clouds white and fluffy
  rise far above the river.

---

* Zhuluo 諸羅 was the name of Jiayi 嘉義 prior to being renamed in 1787.

At noon the party reaches Puwei Creek, famous for its dense banyan trees. Here the party boards a small boat pulled by coolies on the shore. Although Yu has been through this area in years past, he has never before come as on official business; thus this is the first time that he is treated to a ride downriver.

Yu can see the banyan trees planted during the Song Dynasty. Over the course of six centuries the trees have grown to cover the banks of the river, their roots wrapping around each other, in and out, like snakes. At places one tree can stretch over two hundred meters along the banks.

As they glide down river through the town of Hantou, Yu remembers passing by this spot in the river six years ago. The lychees were wonderful, Yu recalls.

They sleep in Xinghua Jun.

FEBRUARY 19

ON THE PUYANG PATH

Spring has come early this year, as it always does in Fujian due to the warm climate. The wheat has already ripened. The wind caresses the fields, makes waves with the grain now waiting for harvesting. The golden glow of the spring sun fills Yu with a feeling of warmth. He delights in this simple pleasure, yet is at once overcome with fear about his long journey ahead. He writes a verse:

> *Days like these,*
> *when I can taste the happiness of a simple farmer,*
> *why must I journey to places far yonder?*

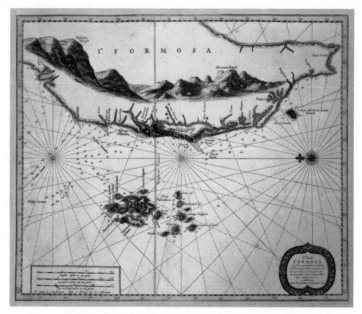

A sea-chart of Penghu (I. Pehoe) and the Taiwan coast.
By Dutch cartographer Pieter Van der Aa (1659-1733)

WU YING AND THE FALL OF PENGHU

From many miles out the road to Quanzhou is flanked with soldiers. They stand at attention in full ceremonial costume. Each soldier holds a two-meter long spear; unwavering, its blade points skyward. The cavalry stand in the background with their bows strung over their backs and a quiver full of arrows with colorful feathers at their side.[2]

It is Quanzhou. It is February 20, 1697. Everyone is awaiting the arrival of Wu Ying, the newly appointed military commander of Fujian's land forces.

The whole village has gathered in anticipation of the general's arrival, crowding the streets and pushing to get a position along the road to catch a glimpse of the man. Yu and his party happen to arrive in Quanzhou today. They too hope to see the famous general. Yu knows that Wu Ying was responsible for the strategy that gave the Qing victory in the battle on Penghu island's which led to the capture of Taiwan. It was Wu's military genius that has made it possible for Yu to travel to Taiwan.[3]

Although he is not expected to arrive until the next day, it will be well worth the wait, for Wu has risen out of complete destitution to become one of the most powerful generals in all of China. As a child Wu was kidnapped by pirates and raised on a secluded island off the Chinese coast. By the time the Ming government collapsed and the Qing marched on Beijing in 1644, Wu had already become an adept sea warrior. He could pilot a ship and wage duels on the high seas, though his status remained that of a pirate. Seeing opportunity to rise to propriety and serve a government, he submitted to the Qing in 1662. The Qing did not immediately give the young pirate turned subservient subject of the emperor an official rank, but rather a lower managerial job on the coast. Even so, Wu took part in many battles to put down the pockets of rebellion in the southern interior and along the coast. Given his naval skills, and the government's need of proficient soldiers, Wu grasped an opportunity that would propel his career to the very heights of the Qing military: he entered service with the Qing Navy commander Shi Lang.[4]

Under Shi Lang, Wu fought to exterminate the Zheng family camped on Taiwan. Shi Lang had been pulled out of retirement by emperor Kangxi to head the Qing Navy in a final assault on the Zhengs who had fled to Taiwan as the last of the Ming resistance in 1661. The Zheng commander-in-chief was none other than Zheng Chenggong, or Koxinga as the Europeans called him, an ambitious and feisty Navy admiral who promptly removed himself to Taiwan after suffering a devastating defeat in Nanjing. Although incompetent on land, Zheng was adroit at sea, frustrating the Qing in their efforts to dislodge him and his subsequent offspring from the island over the course of twenty-two years. Enter Shi Lang. As the emperor told Shi: "Unless you are sent to Taiwan it will never be pacified."[5]

In all his enthusiasm and puissance, Shi Lang led a massive force of over two hundred ships to the Penghu Islands at the end of June 1683, and into a bloody battle, with what Shi Lang called a "bandit mob of over twenty thousand men,"which almost destroyed his fleet. Far outnumbering his adversaries Shi Lang carelessly charged forward, brining his Navy straight into a line of enemy warships. The botched battle became so confusing that Shi Lang's support could not tell foe from friend and fled. As one observer put it, "they stood waiting for the enemy to attack first, then, when the enemy did, they waited for other sailors to fight."[6] The island had been fortified with 12 new gun batteries and mud walls stretching 20 kilometers along the coast and armed with "bandits ready to defend them to the death."Shi Lang barely escaped, taking with him a piece of shot in his right eye.[7] Wu Ying injured his ear.

In a rage at having led such a reckless assault, Shi Lang wanted to vent his incompetence on his captains with a display of beheading. Wu Ying advised against it and suggested a tactic instead, the "Five Petal Plum Blossom Tactic."

"What is the Five Petal Plum Blossom Tactic?"Shi Lang asked.

"Their ships are few and ours are many. We divide into teams of five ships each. Each team attacks one of their ships,"said Wu.

So amused by its simplicity, Shi laughed out loud. "Yes! With such a plan we will certainly defeat them!"he cried. Simple, effective, yet only the pirate-trained mind of Wu conceived of it.[8]

In six days, they returned and put Wu's tactic into practice. As Shi Lang related in one of his more literary memorials to the emperor,"cannon shot and arrows fell like rain. Smoke and flame covered the sky. Fighting dragged on from early morning to late afternoon as our marines fought without regard for their own lives."

Outnumbered, outgunned, and facing imminent defeat at the hands of the Qing Navy, Zheng troops packed gunpowder into the holds of their own ships and blew themselves up. Some twenty two Zheng ships were disposed of this way. Shi Lang said that the Zheng Navy suffered twelve thousand casualties, 134 ships sunk or burned, and 165 officers surrendered with 4,853 troops. "What needed to be burned was burned. Those that needed to be killed were killed...bodies covered the surface of the sea."[9]

For all the havoc wrought on the bandits, and for the tremendous victory gained by the genius of his strategy, Wu received little in return. Shi commended himself for the tactic in the memorial to the emperor on the battle, while Wu only received mention as a captain who "led a battalion" and "killed over three thousand bandits."[10] Wu did get an audience with the emperor the next year, however, and a blunt question from him as well: "Do you have anything to say?" Wu gave a suggestion on governing Taiwan: "Of the eight thousand troops, I recommend putting half of them to work in the fields." The Son of Heaven told him to write a report on the matter before curtly dismissing him.[11]

Yet Wu must have impressed the emperor, for within twelve years he had been promoted to commander-in-chief of the Fujian army, and the next year he stood at the head of the Qing Navy, one of the most powerful posts in all of China. ♋

"A Chinese or Javanese boat with reed sails and wooden anchors." A print from Jan Huygen van Linschoten's A History of the Navigation to the East Indies published posthumously in 1619.

FEBRUARY 22

XIAMEN

In the morning Yu and his party walk 20 kilometers to Liuwu Dian where they catch a boat to cross the small strait to Xiamen Island. As they push off into the salt water a strong wind creates waves like mountains that pummel the small ship, throwing it back and forth. The water crashes over the top striking three meters up the mast. It is only a short journey, though the worst that Yu has ever experienced on a boat.

Looking back over the narrow sea to the opposite shore, Yu sees that the storm has subsided and the sun casts a refulgent sunset of incandescent colors.

In the cool evening, with high spirits from the magnificent sunset, they walk another 15 kilometers to the Shuixian Temple but find the hostels small and cramped; not even a place to stand, he writes sarcastically. Yu goes up to the Hefeng Temple and sits in meditation until dawn breaks.

FEBRUARY 23

XIAMEN

Yu asks around for a ship and captain to take them across the strait to Taiwan via Penghu. A man from Yu's home province of Zhejiang helps him secure a respectable captain to make the four-day journey to Taiwan.

Yu must also obtain permission from the port authorities to make the trip. Not everyone can travel to Taiwan. In fact, the Qing have tried to keep the island relatively unpopulated in order to minimize administrative costs and lessen the chances of rebellion. In an attempt to create a migratory population, the government did not allow women or families to cross. They hoped that the men would travel to Taiwan during the spring planting and then return to their families after the fall harvest. In this way the population in early Qing Taiwan became that of male laborers dependent on the government for access to their families on the mainland. The government helds the families of these migrant laborers responsible for any crimes the Taiwan traveler happened to commit.

Even under such a system, official permission to cross is not easy to obtain. The would-be traveler must apply for travel papers at the office in their native locality, which must also be approved by maritime authorities on both sides of the Taiwan Strait. These papers could carry heavy costs and perhaps require bribes if the official in charge is not agreeable or finds some fault in the application.

Yu has no trouble obtaining permission. He has official papers from the Fuzhou city government, the highest administrative unit in Fujian. The Xiamen maritime office quickly issues him permission to cross to Taiwan and undertake his mission in search of sulfur.

They cannot sail today, however, as the wind has resumed its bois-terous games, making sailing conditions too dangerous. Yu takes Dong and his nephew to what he has heard to be the best places for adventure: Thousand Rock Crag and Tiger Gorge.

The adventure turns into carefree enjoyment, and Yu remembers the pleasure of traveling and being out in nature, among the mountains and trees. The three happy-go-lucky explorers wander among the rock garden that has grown like a forest. They send the servants for food and picnic on rock tables. Drinking wine Yu notes how happy he is. As evening approaches they wander out of the rock forest on the same path they had come in on, playing games to see who can be the first one out of the park. When they finally emerge, a crescent moon hangs in the sky. The day's scenery gives Yu the inspiration for poem:

> Which night was it
> when the moon was black
> and the wind blew like mad,
> casting the rocks into the sea?
> The clouds moving between the pillars,

and I am among the heavens.
The waterfall spray,
and I am among the earth.
I am looking for the road to return
many times but I am joyfully lost.

FEBRUARY 24
TIGER GORGE, XIAMEN

Yu climbs up Tiger Gorge Rock. The rock stands like a giant drum on the hillside with a chiseled path spiraling upwards. On top of the magnificent rock lies another round rock. In fact, all the rocks on Xiamen are round. They excite Yu into writing a verse:

Many strong rocks, all types together
I climb on top and see a drum.

To one side of Tiger Gorge Rock, Yu sees an old decaying wall with an overgrown path leading inside. He finds the old school where Zheng Chenggong's son, Zheng Jing, once studied. Now there is nothing, only the noise of the insects.

Yu has little admiration for the young Zheng, calling him "a spoiled despot" with "no strategy or plan."[12] In fact, in his final days, Zheng Chenggong also cared little for his son, demanding his execution for what was deemed an incestuous affair with his younger brother's wet nurse. The would be executioners sent for Zheng Jing hesitated and defied the order, calling it unreasonable. Almost a breach of loyalty, the kind that would have sent Zheng Chenggong into a fit or rage had he not promptly died. An uncle immediately tried to seize power, which caused a split in forces leading, as a contemporary observer said, "many generals to surrender to the Qing. We gave them rank and honor and, increasingly by the day, they gave us their loyalty."[13]

Neither Yu nor Zheng Chenggong, however, gave Zheng Jing the credit he deserves. Zheng Jing maneuvered within the Zheng family politics and rose to assert himself as the commander-in-chief. Within a few years he felt he had such a stronghold over the island and surrounding seas that he took to calling himself the "King of Taiwan."[14] In Chinese, he named his new kingdom Dongning, or the Eastern Peace. As he wrote to the Qing who requested his surrender, "we are far off in the sea and have established our own country called Dongning. It is separate from [China's] territory. Here we have created a whole new universe."[15] The Qing respected the establishment of Zheng Jing's new country, referring to it as Dongning and to Zheng the ruler of Dongning, and even sending Shi Lang to conquer "Dongning," not "Taiwan." Although the Dongning king requested recog-nition and status equal to Japan and the Philippines, the Qing would not consent because Zheng was Chinese and had established Chinese insti-tutions in his new country.

MARCH 8
GULANG YU

Yu hurt his back hiking. The day they returned he had to be carried home. He cannot move and has been lying in bed for almost two weeks now. Although his back is still sore, the wind has stopped and the ship's captain orders them to hurry on board so they can sail.

The ship hardly gets out of the harbor before heavy rains crash into the sea. When the downpour stops, strong winds rock the ship back and forth for three days and three nights without rest. Yu cannot write, nor can he think. He is painfully, overwhelmingly, violently sick.

When the storm does pass, Yu climbs out of his cabin for fresh air and to look around. He sees the Gulang Yu islet, the spot of land at the tip of the southern peninsula; the spot where the great military commander Zheng Chenggong led just eighteen loyal troops out of Xiamen after learning his father had surrendered to the Qing in 1647; the spot where Zheng found his motivation to form his own army and to continue to resist the Qing. It was here, on Gulang Yu, that Zheng first gathered a few hundred soldiers and took to attacking and pirating his family's ships in order to pay them. Yu recalls a story that a Zheng family servant protested, crying "how can you take these ship without family consent." The fervid fiery Zheng Chenggong screamed, "Who do you take me for!?" and ordered the servant's execution.[16]

Zheng Chenggong, also known as Koxinga, fled from China and drove the Dutch from Taiwan in 1662, only to die from malaria three months later. This portrait is believed to be the only surviving contemporary depiction of Zheng Chenggong.

ZHENG CHENGGONG (KOXINGA)

Zheng Chenggong has been held responsible for putting Taiwan on the Chinese map. History has been kind to Zheng, even if Yu considers him an outlaw and rebel. Yet both know Zheng as the man who brought Taiwan into China's national interest, raised it from a far off rock in the sea to a frontier worth occupying. Yu knows that without Zheng, his journey might never have begun.

Better known in the west as Koxinga*, Zheng was a self-interested and vicious military commander acting as the last of the Ming resistance when the Manchus swept China and consolidated their Qing Dynasty in the 1650s. Although Zheng held almost all the southern coast at one time, his base remained in Xiamen. As one of the Ming generals wrote in a letter to Zheng that argued against removing to Taiwan: "Xiamen is the root and

* "Koxinga" is the European bastardization of *Guo-xing-ye*, or Lord of the Imperial Surname, the title bestowed upon Zheng as a child by the Ming Emperor.

Taiwan but a small leaf. If there is no Xiamen then there is no root, so how can we even have the leaves!? ...Fleeing to Taiwan is like taking a backward step. '[17]

Zheng eventually took the giant backward step to Taiwan, but at one time he had thousands of war junks anchored in Xiamen and scores more scattered up the coast. It was then, in the 1650s, that Zheng Chenggong possessed a fleet the Jesuit Ricci said, "the sight of which inspires tremendous terror.'[18] It also performed admirably, winning twenty-seven of thirty-five battles with the Qing and nearly obliterating the Manchu Navy twice. In 1655, at the height of his power, Zheng commanded some 250,000 soldiers and 2,300 ships. Like his seagoing father before him, Zheng had the skill, ability, and determination to rule the coast. He had grown up climbing the masts of his father's massive war junks and knew what it took to lead a great Navy. Here, on the beaches of Xiamen, he disciplined his soldiers to go without shoes, enabling them to maneuver quickly in the sand. Although Zheng enforced this rule with severe punishments—he was even known to take away honors if he caught an officer wearing shoes—it led to brilliant success in battles on the beach. The Qing armies, with their heeled riding boots got stuck in the sand and became then easy prey for the agile Zheng forces. As one contemporary commented, "no wonder the Qing lost every battle on the beach!'[19]

Such tactics figured prominently in Zheng's siege of Fuzhou in 1656. He occupied the island of Minan at the mouth of the Minjiang river and moved in on the capital city where he annihilated eight large banner forces and killed three of the Qing's top generals. Even after his defeat at Nanjing, Zheng leveled a morale boosting attack on Chongming Island near Shanghai, gaining an easy victory with the strength of his Navy. He inflicted such carnage on the Qing Navy that a contemporary European historian recorded that "for many weeks after the terrible catastrophe the beaches of Haimuen were covered with rotting bodies and naval spoils that the flux and surge of the sea would daily cast on the shores.'[20] Those who survived suffered physical mutilation at the hands of Zheng who shipped them back to the Qing when he had finished mutilating their flesh, an act which Ricci noted was "to show the tartars that they cannot expect any peace from him."[21] Indeed, the Dutch even said that the Qing "had more work in trying to exterminate this one man than they experienced in subduing millions of people."[22]

Yet the Qing eventually did succeed in dealing with Zheng when he tried to take his campaign inland in a siege at Nanjing. The fight of the southern capital stands as one of those apposite battles in history where the fate of a country and millions of people get ironed out in an afternoon. The battle of Nanjing was the decisive defeat of the lingering Ming loyalists in China and the consolidation of Manchu power in the establishment of their Qing Dynasty. But more significantly for the story of Taiwan and Yu's ability to travel there, it sealed Zheng's by fate sending him scurrying from China and off to Taiwan to lick his wounds, so to speak.

Within two weeks of arriving at the gates of Nanjing, Zheng was scurrying back down river with less than half of his army still alive. From there the momentum of defeat did not cease. The Qing cut off his supply lines leaving Zheng with a severe shortage of food and munitions. When sacking towns and cities he would force the residents to feed his troops and provide them with provisions. His soldiers got so accustomed to pillaging that Zheng, trying not to lose the support of the people, wrote in his military law that soldiers "can take food and provisions but cannot rape."[23] Furthermore, constant military pressure from the Manchus on Zheng's tiny kingdom in Xiamen made trading operations difficult. In short, Zheng needed a larger base that was safe from the Qing, had ample provisions, and was positioned on the major trade routes.

Given Zheng's situation, Taiwan appeared the logical place in which to retreat. As the Dutch put it, reflecting on Zheng's move, "Formosa was the only place where there was the least hope of safety." Zheng certainly thought so. The urging of a spy, in possession of stolen Dutch maps along with tales of the weakness of the unpopular Dutch, only deepened his resolve. And so Zheng left China, "hiding his wife and children and all their moveable goods in his junks, and remove from one island to another, "as his Dutch contemporaries observed. Zheng sailed his several hundred war junks, with some twenty-five thousand battle hardened soldiers, into present day Tainan on April 30, 1661, destined to become the first Chinese administration on Taiwan.[24]   og

I implore, do not cross to Taiwan,
    it will take you to the gates of hell.
Thousands go but never one to return.
    Whether they live or die, no one can tell.

Those who are single, off they go
    with no parents or loved ones to stall,
just chose an auspicious day, so
    out the door with no tears to fall.

All the ships line up to sail.
    Passengers load up in the hull
waiting for a wind or gale,
    sometimes many months without the gull.

When the winds are right then they are off,
    just three days and two nights to the Taiwan shore.
To disembark, out comes the skiff
    demanding cash or they row no more.

DIRGE OF THE TAIWAN STRAIT

UNKNOWN POET

PART 2

The Crossing

渡

海

MATZOU

Formosan Boat.

Champan Chinese Boat.

Nineteenth-century French depiction of boats in the Taiwan Strait. Both these types of vessels were used for the journey between Xiamen and Taiwan Fu.

A Dutch print of Mazu, the sea goddess Chinese fishermen ask to watch over them and keep them safe.

The Crossing

MATCH 11

DADAN ISLAND

"There is no wind and we cannot move," Yu writes. They are anchored at Dadan Island, just 10 kilometers out of Xiamen. It is a safe place to stop before heading into the tempestuous open waters of the Taiwan Strait. Twelve other ships are also anchored here waiting for the wind so that they might hoist their sails and move out to sea and across the strait.

Yu rests peacefully, but Dong cannot get used to the rocking of the boat. He falls to his knees and throws up in violent heaves.

MARCH 13

TAIWAN STRAIT

At dawn Yu awakens to the beating of drums and banging of the gong. The breeze has finally picked up and the sailors on Yu's ship are the first to feel it. In order to alert the sailors on the other ships anchored nearby that it is time to sail, they begin to beat the drum and sound the gong.

On the whole of the China coast, the Taiwan Strait is the only place to see such a practice. Here the wind will blow in such overwhelming gusts that ships cannot sail, or the wind will not blow at all, becalming them for days or weeks at a time. Sailors have learned to pass the time, to sleep and hide themselves in the lower cabins until the breeze comes. As they wait, other ships hoping to make the passage from Fujian to Taiwan, or Taiwan to Fujian, also wait. Unlike the small number of ships going to the Ryukyu Islands in the north, or to the Philippines in the south, every day many ships set sail for Taiwan. When the wind does come, the sailors rush to put up the sails and alert the other ships anchored nearby by banging the drums and sounding the gong.

When Yu climbs on deck they have already sailed out of the Dadan Island bay. At noon they stop near another island with a reddish colored mountain. Yu sends his servant to ask the captain why they have stopped. "We have no wind and can't sail," the captain informs him.

"Where are we," Yu asks.

"Liaoluo, Jinmen Island," The captain responds.

By evening Yu can still see the same red hill as if it were upon them. The wind hardly blows.

"I am afraid of the wind," Yu reflects. "But I am more afraid of no wind." The ship cannot use its oars on the open sea and the strange fact that one must rely on only a large piece of reed to sail thousands of miles becomes disturbingly evident to the once landlocked passengers.

During the first watch, Yu awakens to the howling of the wind. Below he can hear the waves crashing against the side of the boat. Dong is sick and moans in concert with the tossing waves.

That night they cross the Red Ditch, a trench in the ocean where currents converge. Its deep hue is reddened by the sun during the day.[1]

MARCH 14

PENGHU

At daylight Yu can see the Black Ditch. It is a giant ditch scaring the ocean floor, creating currents that can drag flat-bottomed boats and wind-driven ships off course, sometimes even to the depths of the sea. Under storms and high winds the Black Ditch can run in every direction,[2] and among local sailors it is known as the "most dangerous spot in the sea."[3] Indeed, it has pulled countless people to their death and spawned tales of terror in Fujian. An unknown poet captured the feeling in his "Dirge of the Taiwan Strait," a poem to his friend who set out to cross the sea:

> I implore, do not cross to Taiwan,
>   it will take you to the gates of hell.
> Thousands go but never one to return.
>   Whether they live or die, no one can tell.[4]

In the days of wooden rudders and sailboats, the Black Ditch would quickly take command of a ship and spin it out of control. During storms or on a restless sea, whirlpools would form and drag ships to their doom. Official records from 1729 to 1838 registered some eighty-six military and government ships that sank in the Taiwan Strait, pulling thousands of hapless military and civilian officials to their death. The legends say that their spirits haunt the strait, demanding from fishermen a human sacrifice every three years. "If you don't comply then the spirits will haunt you for another three years," the fishermen say.[5]

But most of those crossing are unregistered civilian boats and do not make the official records.[6] Many on board are immigrants seeking passage to a better life on Taiwan soil. They stow away on a vessel with hopes of making it safely to an island with plenty of land and water. But the immigration operations are often run by "pirates and other bad characters of the water world," say tales, who charge by the head and stuff as many people as possible into the ship's hold, board it up and refuse to show them the sky. Accounts of these overloaded ships tell of setting off at night and running into waves and wind that capsize the ship. "All on board go to the fishes' bellies," according to the tales.[7]

Even if the ship is fortunate enough to avoid the danger of the Black Ditch and make it to Taiwan, the captain, fearing arrest for smuggling, "dumps his passengers on the coastal rocks." At low tide the people "walk in and get caught in quicksand." At high tide "they are swept out to sea to become fish food."[8] Or worse, greedy captains just throw their human cargo overboard into the middle of the sea, stealing their personal items and other goods to take back to market to sell. Qing official Lan Dingyuan, unable to stop the trends, wrote a poem of lamentation for those dying in the strait:

> Shackled up in a line,
> everyone with their own tale
> their bodies weak and frail.
> If they touch land they must go to jail.
> So dumb, yet so sanguine.[9]

Yu's ship stays upright but everyone is repulsed by the stench permeating from the Black Ditch, and they fear the sea snakes frolicking around the ship will attack. Yu says there are black snakes with red stripes and snakes with two heads that jump in and out of the water like killer sea serpents. The captain throws paper money as an offering into the water calling for the snakes to be gone.

Then, all is safe. The Penghu Islands appear as a thin line on the horizon, "right where the sky meets the water." Yu is so awed by the scene that he forgets his fears and writes a dreamy poem of the sea:

> The great sea and only a small ship.
> Algae beneath
> a uniform blue sky.

Wind all about
and waves of a thousand white mountains
where the earth meets the sky
standing like a thin line.
The ship rises to heights and sinks down to depths.
*Don't mistake these words for the words of a fool.**

The wind is calm again and Yu's ship is forced to drift. They sit just 30 meters out of the harbor. By the time they finally enter and drop anchor darkness has fallen.

---

* Yu is referring to a poem by Zhuang Zi describing the vastness of the sea. Later commentators criticized Zhuang Zi for exaggerating and called him a fool.

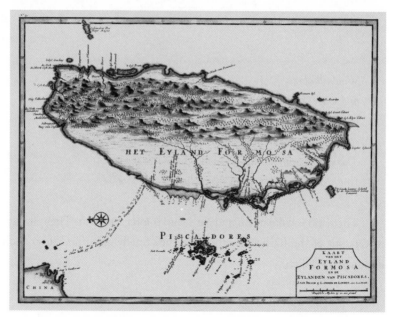

Taiwan (Formosa) and Penghu (Piscadores) by Dutch bookseller Jan van Braam, 1726. The detail of rivers and coast are quite accurate.

THE DUTCH AT PENGHU

When the Dutch arrived in the Far East in 1622, they came to Penghu. They came as merchants, or, as one chronicler put it, "to trade with [China], and procure goods to take over to Japan, that they might force the Portuguese out of it."[10] In 1602, as the Dutch republic began to nurture its political power in the form of mercantilism, the Dutch East India Company was formed with the aim of coordinating companies competing for trade in Asia and act as an arm of the Dutch state against Spain and Portugal. Both Spain and Portugal had trading monopolies with China and controlled commerce throughout the Asian seas—the Spanish in Manila, the Portuguese in Macao. The Dutch wanted a share. They set up headquarters in Batavia (modern-day Jakarta) in the early seventeenth century but remained intensely focused on what they believed to be the most lucrative place in the world, China. As one of the company's early governor-generals commented, "there is no people in the world who can serve us better than the Chinese."[11] Under such conviction, the governor set out to occupy Penghu from where he could intercept Portuguese commerce between Macao and Japan, and Chinese and Spanish trade between Xiamen and Manila. Such a geographical position also allowed him to conduct periodic raids on Fujian to "induce the Chinese to trade by force or from fear."

The Portuguese had sailed by in 1544 and called the islands the Pescadores, or "fishermen," in honor of the Chinese fishermen camped out on the grassy islands. The Portuguese wrote a report on the islands and sent it back to Europe. The word soon spread and the Dutch, having failed to drive the Portuguese out of Macau, began to take a keen interest in the islands as a means to break into the Chinese market. It was from here that the Dutch launched their raids on the Fujian coast after their failed attempts to trade with the Chinese who, as Lieutenant Elie Ripon says, treated them "as if we were chicken or children, and informed us to go away and go back to Holland where we came from." The Dutch did not take the rejection lightly, especially Ripon who had come as a mercenary. He noted with great glee that "I have made them feel the bill of the chicken, because as soon as we had put the fortress in order, Commander Reijersen, Captain Christan Schelling and I returned with the fleet to the coast of China and started to set everything aflame and maim everybody we met all along the coast from the provinces of Canton and Chinchau [Fujian] as far as the islands of Cheshan [Zhoushan] on land and on sea: and we have done so for two and a half years. We have destroyed many villages and castles and a great number of their ships which they call junks."[12]

At the mouth of the harbor on the main Penghu island, the Dutch built a four-cornered fort with twenty guns on the walls and another seven guns mounted around the fort's perimeter. For the construction of the fort they imported some 1,500 Chinese, bound them together by twos and forced them to carry baskets of dirt to the construction site. With food rations of one bowl of rice a day, almost all died, many of starvation. The 270 survivors were shipped off to Batavia in the Indies and sold into slavery. As the registers explain: "Only 137 made it to Batavia, the rest couldn't take it and died or we threw them to the sea."[13] The Chinese authorities did not take lightly to such practices. So much so that two years later they decided that the "Red Hair Barbarians" posed a security threat, and refused to grant them trading rights unless they retreated to Taiwan. Commented one Dutch observer, "we were the more easily persuaded to do this on being told that the Chinese were preparing fifteen thousand fire ships, war junks and stone junks to fill up the bay of Penghu."[14] The Dutch packed up their castle piece by piece in 1624, and promptly removed themselves to Taiwan.   ☞

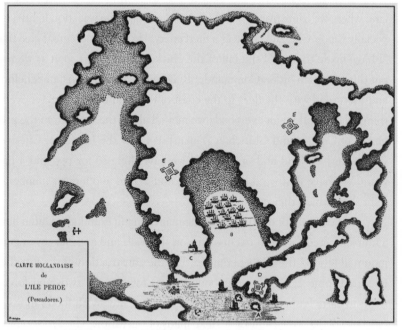

A 1670 Dutch print of Penghu. The fort at the bottom is the Dutch fort.
The other two on the island are Chinese forts.

MARCH 15

PENGHU

Yu takes a landing craft to shore. The sand is soft and no vegetation grows on the low coastline. The whole island is barren of trees. The island is barren of everything but long grass and sand. Yu sinks up to his knees when he steps onto the beach.

When the Dutch were here they could find no fresh water on the island except what they referred to as "a few small wells, which are somewhat brackish in the dry season." Indeed, the Dutch were "greatly bothered...that these islands are very sandy, infertile, and devoid of wood and stone." All their provisions came from the Taiwan mainland.[15]

Yu finds some 2,000 troops stationed on the Penghu islands. They are the Qing's first large standing army on Penghu in Chinese history. "To protect Taiwan, Penghu is the most important," Yu says.

The Yuan Dynasty did put officials on Penghu in 1281, making the islands a part of Fujian provincial protectorate. That lasted a hundred years, until the Ming took power and decided that the island station only provided pirates with supplies on their periodic raids. Apparently, the Beijing rulers failed to consider the islands might come to serve as a pirate base, which they did, allowing pirates to "terrorize the whole China coast, laying waste to provinces, towns and villages, and rendering navigation along that part of the coast impracticable," as the Dutch wrote.[16]

Penghu also became the determining factor in the Qing war against the Zhengs. After Zheng general Liu Guoxuan suffered the devastating defeat on Penghu at the hands of Shi Lang, he knew the Zheng kingdom on Taiwan could hold out no longer. General Liu caught a small craft to Taiwan to meet with the political authority of the Zheng government whom, upon learning of the defeat and decimation of the Zheng forces, began to entertain a fanciful plan to invade the Philippines where "ridiculous priests cheat the foolish people," as Zheng official Haung Liangji put it. "Now that Penghu is lost and Taiwan in danger we should use both our warships and our commercial ships to remove civilians and soldiers from the hillside, sailing down to conquer Luzon as our new base."[17] Liu disliked the plan and feared the Qing would pursue. With 90 percent of his troops killed or having deserted, and the Qing able to stage attacks from Penghu just hours out from Taiwan, he disagreed adamantly. For twenty days they quibbled among themselves before surrendering on July 27, 1683. The last Zheng ruler, Zheng Keshuang, shaved his head, donned the Qing robes and went to Beijing where he received an honorary yet ineffectual title.

The fishermen Yu meets on the island remember the war. It was only fourteen years ago. One of them gives Yu a shark. When Yu's servant cuts it open he finds seven baby sharks inside. Although Yu had heard others deny that sharks lay eggs, he has finally made the discovery for himself that sharks give live birth. Back on the ship Yu also experiences phosphorus glowing in the water for the first time.

At midnight a light breeze picks up and the captain steers the ship out of the harbor.

MARCH 16

LU-ER-MEN

A light westerly wind fills the ship's sails. Yu watches the color of the sea lighten and the Penghu islands slowly disappear behind him. Over the bow, the Taiwan mountains appear, slowly rising above the sea. Within five hours they have reached the seven lumps of green earth that form the harbor Lu-er-men, the port of entry to Taiwan.

Stretching some five kilometers from north to south along Taiwan's western coast, the small islands of shoals and sand is suspended miles at sea off the Taiwan shore. Home to fishermen and sparse vegetation it provides a natural wave break creating what Yu calls "another sea from the one outside." When storms rage and the ocean attacks everything with malice—when even the mouth of the harbor is hidden in water and foam—the sea inside remains calm and tranquil. The *Taiwan Fu Gazetteer* published in 1694 noted that "there is no better piece of coast line protection."[18]

Over a hundred years after Yu, this numinous wonder of nature silted up when a shortsighted official stuffed the mouth with dirt to keep out the foreign ships. This came with the added bonus of choking the harbor and keeping the mountain runoffs in. In 1823, the summer rains brought torrential floods flushing mud and sand into a harbor unable to drain itself. Three quarters of the once sea-sized harbor silted up with fresh dirt. People began to put up houses on the land and turn it into a fish market. In a report to the emperor, military general Guanxi said, "we can no longer sail into Taiwan Fu to deliver military supplies...once a buffer from attack, we can no longer rely on the harbor for protection."[19] By 1842 the harbor completely filled in with earth to become part of the island's landmass.

Today, Yu makes no orphic judgments about geographical changes or even the threat of foreigners. Today, rather, Yu composes a poem to express his awe of the famous harbor.

Iron sand piled firm in seven mounds,
    like a whale striking the water, waves abound.
Any ship is hard to come,
    this is what heaven has created as Lu-er-men.

Yu's ship is not the only one to reach Taiwan today. A number of vessels have lined up at the entrance, waiting for official clearance from the harbor patrol. Inspections often turn up ships attempting illegal passage or arriving with illegal cargo. If a ship does not have the proper permission forms it is turned away and not allowed to enter the harbor. Unless the captain is quick-witted and the inspection guard willing, in which case a financial transaction takes place and the ship is rushed through. Such a transaction must also happen at the time of embarkation, otherwise the ship will not be allowed out of the harbor. Often these transactions occur off duty. The time and place of embarkation determined and the under-table fees paid. Then, in secret, the guard will let the ship pass through his inspection.

The patrol is also checking for smugglers. All firearms and gunpowder are banned, and the export of rice from Taiwan is prohibited. For a fee it is said that the guards will look the other way. Captains must compile cargo manifests and crew rolls, and the inspectors will take careful stock of the goods and people on board. For those that they find, they compare the detailed crew roll description with the person they have in front of them. Anyone on board who does not fit a description is returned. Or a sum can be slipped to the guard for him to kindly ignore the discrepancy. Likewise, if a ship arrives with more people than its papers say it should have, it will be turned away. Or, if it comes with less souls that it started out with, the captain may try to explain the phenomenon by telling the guards one was lost to the sea. If he is not smooth enough with his tongue, the captain may be forced to add weight to the guard's purse or return along the same sea route from whence he came.

Each inspection takes time and Yu's ship is forced to wait at the edge of the open sea. The wind suddenly picks up creating a giant surge that rocks the ship. The sea moving in on them forms the biggest waves Yu has ever seen. When their turn finally comes and the patrol sees Yu's rank and documentation, they are immediately waved through. The captain follows a lead boat into the harbor. The sea is not rough inside but the water is shallow with sand that Yu describes "winds this way and that." Although their destination lies only 5 kilometers away by a straight line, the parts of the harbor deep enough for large ships to pass through do not run in straight lines. They must steer a route that takes them some 15 kilometers in a jagged course back and forth across the harbor. The Dutch also found it "not without much inconvenience," marking it as 11 feet of water, "which was also very crooked so that no large vessels could enter."[20]

This inconvenient characteristic has given the harbor a strategic advantage: a direct attack would be foiled by the shallow sand, beaching unsuspecting ships. The *Taiwan Fu Gazetteer* calls the harbor "very dangerous [for ships to sail into], but easy to protect."[21] When Zheng Chenggong came to fight the Dutch on Taiwan, the Dutch purposely left the mouth of Lu-er-men harbor unguarded hoping to draw in an unsuspecting Zheng for what he would mistake as an easy assault on the forts. Zheng was supposed to run aground on the shallow harbor but, as the tale is told in seventeenth century Tainan, upon approaching the harbor Zheng called for an altar on his ship's deck where he knelt down with incense and prayed: "Heavens have pity and rise the tides to help my ships advance. Leave no obstacle in my path and guide my troops safely ashore."[22] The tide rose especially high that day, as high as 10 meters, allowing Zheng to sail his junks safely into Lu-er-men and level a frontal attack on the Dutch who could only sit like the "melancholy spectators" they called themselves, watching "the enemy taking full advantage of the opportunity." In honor of heaven's service, Zheng renamed the Dutch castle Anping, or Quiet Peace.

The Dutch did not go peacefully, however. Zheng's several hundred war junks with some twenty-five thousand battle-hardened soldiers arrived on April 30, 1661, giving the 1,140 Dutch in their castle a somber fright. Over the next four hours Zheng goaded himself in a debouch display of his massive naval power against two Dutch war ships. Zheng's captain promptly opened fire on the Hector, the larger of the two war ships come to greet the first line of Chinese junks, creating, as the Dutch described, "such a terrible explosion that it caused the windows of the castle to shake; and when the smoke had cleared away, neither the Hector nor the junks which had been nearest to it could be seen." The results of this mismatched little battle only gave Zheng a Dutch ceasefire but sunk a number of his ships and killed over one thousand of his troops.[23]

MARCH 17

CHIKAN, TAIWAN FU

The Goddess Mazu has delivered Yu safely. All the sailors of the strait will pray to the sea goddess, asking her to watch over them and protect them. They say that if a ship is in danger it can call on Mazu and receive a response from her—either soldiers from the heavens will descend to protect the ship, or Mazu herself will cast her aegis over the sailors. The stories say that if a round light appears on the mast on a dark night then the crossing will fail and the ship sink to the bottom of the sea. They call it the Mazu fire and all past history and experience has confirmed the results. To guard against such catastrophe every ship carries a Mazu stick, by which the fire can burn. Sailors use the stick to beat the side of the ship and drive away sea creatures.

Mazu has always been a mystery. Yu says the stories reveal that she was a real person born in Putian, Fujian, the daughter of a Mr. Lin. As a child she had special powers and in her dreams would fly to the sea to rescue drowning sailors. She never married and after her death her spirit would often appear. Coastal residents in Zhejiang, Fujian, Penghu and Taiwan built temples to offer their prayers to her. In the Ming dynasty she was named and honored as a concubine of the emperor of heaven. After Shi Lang's successful attack on Penghu he anchored at one of the islands and went to pray at the temple. He saw the goddess and she was wet from the waist down. Shi remembers seeing her beside him as they fought Zheng forces and believes he succeeded because of the gods. His deism only strengthened when his army of twenty-five thousand drew sufficient water from a dry well. From Shi Lang's report, Emperor Kangxi elevated Mazu to the status of Queen.[24]

Mazu not only protected Yu and his ship but she delivered them swiftly. It took a day and a half to sail from Xiamen to Taiwan, just under a day from Xiamen to Penghu, and half a day from Penghu to Taiwan. But the wind was favorable for Yu and his party. If the wind did not blow it could take ten days just to move the distance that usually takes just an hour. Or worse, sometimes the east wind is too strong and ships can't enter Lu-er-men, forcing them back to Penghu. If it is a dark night and the captain can't find the harbor at Penghu, his ship can be stranded or forced to return all the way to Xiamen.

Yu asks about the other twelve ships that had set out with them from Xiamen. He is told that only half have arrived. In the subsequent days, Yu will make the journey to shore many times to inquire at the harbor patrol office about the other ships. It will be another eight days before eleven of the twelve ships arrive, and over ten days before the last one comes in safely.

Such a disparity in time perplexes Yu. He pesters an official to explain this phenomenon. "The wind," the official answers.

"But we all left on the same day and took the same route. Why will others come in so much later?" presses Yu.

"The wind on the sea is uncertain. Two ships will never have the same experience, just a small difference between them and the two ships will be miles apart. It is not good luck or bad luck, but rather as if the gods control the outcome. We cannot assign linear values to the speed of the ships," the official responds.

In order to get to the shore and back to make his calls, Yu has bought a landing craft. However, the landing craft can only take him halfway to dry land before the sandy bottom rises to within a few inches of the water's surface and the boat cannot pass. In order to make the rest of the journey to shore without getting wet Yu rides in an ox pulled cart. Like rickshaw boys waiting on the dock, the oxcart drivers line the shore and come out to meet the landing crafts from the ships. They pull their passengers over the shallow water to whatever point on the coastline they wish.

Even after the new experience of the ox cart and arriving on land, Yu cannot shake his seasickness. "Now, I lie on the bed or lean against a chair but I still feel I am at sea." His head is splitting apart, and he remembers being on the ship and getting "thrown about all day as if it were an earthquake."

After two days he feels better and goes out to make calls on local officials. He meets with the Taiwan Fu magistrate, the military general in charge of the Taiwan garrisons, the Zhuluo magistrate, and the Fengshan magistrate. He also runs into an old friend who thinks that Yu has just dropped from the sky. Together they tour Fort Provintia, the second of the two Dutch forts built in Taiwan Fu.

Seventeenth-century Dutch engraving of the war between Zheng Chenggong and the
Dutch. The Chinese archers, pictured on the right, wrought considerable damage on
Dutch forces.

THE CHIKAN FORT
AND ZHENG CHENGGONG'S WAR
AGAINST THE DUTCH

Under the Qing, Fort Provintia has become the Chikan Building, or
"Red Roof," named after the aborigine tribe choused out of their land.
Or, it was named for the height of the ground above the water—no one
remem-bers.

The fort was built at Chikan, right on the water's edge and across the
harbor from the main fort, Zeelandia. The Dutch acquisition of this land
was a ruse as the aborigines occupying the fertile ground did not want to give
it up. Although largely believed to be fictitious, the story goes that the crafty
Dutch told them they only needed a plot the size of a cowhide and were
willing to pay any amount for it. Thinking their European colonizers had
come to swindle themselves out of their money, the aborigines agreed only
to watch the Dutch cut up the cow hide into narrow strips and mark off a

large plot with the insulting words, "this is one cow hide!" Here, in the
cowhide-sized plot, the European's put up Fort Provintia.[25]

The decision to build came in 1652 after what company officials called
a "treacherous attempt" by the Chinese inhabitants on the island "to upset
the Company's authority in Formosa." As the Dutch themselves told it,
some four thousand to five thousand Chinese "longing for liberty...under-
took a dangerous revolt; although the greater number were mere peasants,
some of them armed, but the majority with only sticks and bamboos as their
weapons. Therefore, with the faithful Formosan natives as allies, the Neth-
erlanders soon subdued them; shooting a few, and easily putting to flight
those who were not trained in the art of war." They attacked the Chinese
rebel force, killing eighteen hundred and capturing a great number, the
chief of whom was, as the Dutch records indicate, "roasted alive before a fire
in Taiwan, dragged behind a horse through the town, and head stuck on a
pole." As the battle wore on some 120 Dutch led 600 "Christian Formosans"
into the field and adroitly killed three thousand Chinese. After fifteen days
of unrest, when all was said and done, four thousand men, five thousand
women and some children had been either slain or captured. The Dutch
suffered "not a single loss." Still, the uprising startled the Dutch who
breathed a sigh of relief that it had "fortunately been discovered, quelled,
and suppressed—for which may the name of the Lord be blessed to all
time!"

They said their prayers over a lightly built four-cornered fort of baked
bricks. It was designed to "keep the Chinese colony and a few ill-disposed
inhabitants under better control." If well garrisoned the fort could put down
an uprising or sudden attack, yet it was much too weak to stand a long term
siege or hold out against cannon fire. Even a governor-general wrote in
hindsight that it "should have been built in a much more massive way from
the beginning." The fact of the matter is it wasn't, and Zheng's army of
twenty-five thousand troops quickly subdued it, "cutting down some of our
soldiers," as Reverend Joannes Kruyf tells. "They seized my eldest son, and
the younger brother of my wife, who had one of his arms cut off."

In truth the company had seriously bollixed the tactical decision of preparation. They refused to believe that Zheng would actually lead an invasion on Taiwan. Batavia Council member Nicolaes Verburgh consistently rebuffed Formosa Governor Fredrick Coyett's warnings of an imminent attack from Zheng. He blocked funds for the colony to rebuild weakening fortifications, citing the need for consolidation. "We find it anything but easy to keep the present garrison in Formosa always up to full strength. We therefore prefer to decrease, rather then increase, it." And later, just one month before Zheng landed at the Dutch doorstep, he declared that "Koxinga would not dare to attack us in Formosa."

Yet Verburgh, who had served as the Formosan Governor from 1650-1653, wrote to the Batavia Council during his term that the threat of Zheng "caused my hair to stand on end through agitation." His change of heart after he left may be explained by his immediate removal of himself from the threat of Koxinga; but there was also something personal between Verburgh and Coyett. Coyett did seem to incur the wrath of all the wrong people, to the extent that he lost the colony. He did try his best, making the case for military reinforcements through repeated complaints that "the defensive position of Formosa was far from satisfactory."

Batavia finally sent twelve ships with six hundred troops under the command of Jan van der Laan. The company chronicler says Laan "acted very strangely" and called him "John Against-all-reason." Coyett managed to antagonize the captain, leading to a horrendous argument that exploded into personal vulgarities. Laan made their quarrel official when he departed for Batavia carrying criminal charges against Coyett for unwarranted "preparations of the Governor and Council to resist the enemy, and the audacity of retaining the soldiers after their natural term of service had expired," among other things. Laan took with him all but two war ships, a "little bark" and a "little yacht." Although he left a reserve of soldiers, they had no command, for the captain refused to leave behind any officers.

Though vulnerable, exposed and ill-equipped to face any attack, Laan continued to lobby against any preparation or the sending of supplies to

Coyett, declaring the news of an attack unfounded, and the Chinese soldiers "little better than poor specimens of very effeminate men." However, when Zheng and his epicene soldiers' ineluctable invasion became clear to the Dutch, the Batavia Council, and even the administrators in Holland, began to cry that "Formosa is lost."

Zheng landed at Chikan in late April 1661, and camped out on an open field with his cannons poised and some twelve thousand men sprawled out around the hills. He had sent the other half of his army out to aborigine villages to find food and begin his system of military colony farming. The Dutch, happily stocked with provisions for six months, drew up initial proposals that would either pay off Zheng to leave Taiwan, or give them rights to continue to use the island to trade freely. When presented with such requests, a pompous and dressed up Zheng flatly rejected them: "Hitherto this island had always belonged to China, and the Dutch had doubtless been permitted to live there, seeing that the Chinese did not require it for themselves; but requiring it now, it was only fair that the Dutch strangers, who came from far regions, should give way to the masters of the island."

The Dutch envoys, however, did not agree with Zheng's interpretations of history: " Formosa did not belong to China, but to the company; for by a formal contract drawn up with the grandees of China, they had left the Pescadores and taken possession of Formosa; therefore Koxinga could have no right or pretence of claim to it." At this point Zheng pointed towards the Dutch fort and yelled: "My smart boys will attack it, conquer it, and demolish it in such a way that not one stone will remain standing. If I wish to set my forces to work, then I am able to move Heaven and Earth; wherever I go, I am destined to win. Therefore take warning, and think the matter well over." With that Zheng refused to continue the conversation—feigning language differences—and told the envoy he would give them until eight o'clock the next morning. If they were to stay and fight, the Dutch should not trouble with further delib-erations but unfurl the blood-flag. The envoy solemnly withdrew, and after a sleepless night of heated discussion about how to proceed, the Hollanders, on the morning of May 4, flew a large blood red flag from the top of the castle, rekindling hostilities that would drag on for another nine months.

If Zheng had listened more to his generals and exercised his military sense the battle might have ended quickly, the Dutch disgraced for their incestuous squabbles, and the island comfortably in Chinese hands. Yet what ensued over the next year was another one of Zheng's brilliant shows of poor military planning. In late May a determined Zheng had his troops surround the Zeelandia castle but he remained at a loss on how to finish the siege. His forces outnumbered the Dutch twenty-five to one yet he continually made tactical blunders: underestimating the power of Dutch guns and putting his troops in direct range of their fire; falling victim to blind raids from the Dutch storming out of the castle gates and spiking Chinese guns; letting cannons and horses get stolen from under his nose. There they sat until the following January before Dutch deserters informed Zheng of low moral and gave hints of the castle's weak spots. Zheng pulled all his mental and physical resources together to build three large batteries with twenty-eight guns. On February 1, 1662, before any cannon balls flew, the Dutch surrendered on terms that sacrificed some 471,000 florins in treasure to their Chinese conquerors, but allowed them to leave the island with full honors, "armed to the teeth and with flying banners."[26]   CB

From the north, Taiwan connects to Zhejiang and Jiangsu. From the south, it connects to Guangdong and Guanxi. The island stretches for thousands of miles; the mountains are high and jagged; the harbors curve in and out. This is the protection for Jiangsu, Zhejiang, Fujian and Guangdong.

SHI LANG, QING NAVY ADMIRAL

PART 3

Taiwan Fu

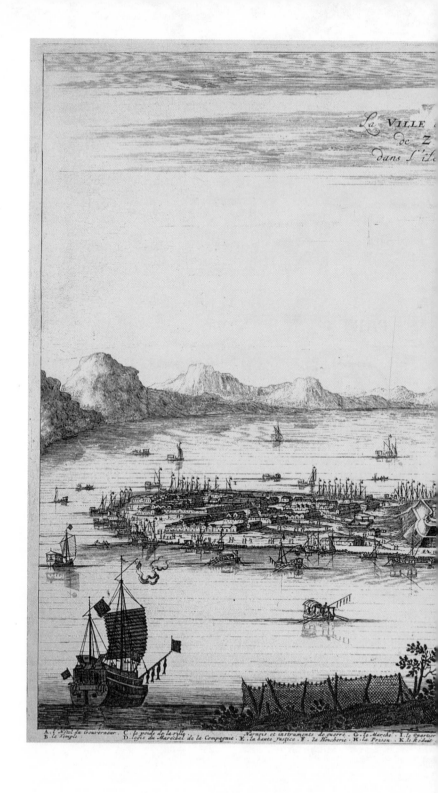

La VILLE
de Z
dans L'île

A. l'Hôtel du Gouverneur. C. la porte de la ville. Harnois et instruments de guerre. G. le Marché. I. le Quartier
B. le Temple. D. logis du Maréchal de la Compagnie. F. la haute justice. F. la Boucherie. H. la Prison. K. le Réduit

ÂTEAU
A
OVAN

*The Dutch Fort Zeelandia at Taiwan Fu in full commercial swing. First
published in Amsterdam in 1670.*

臺灣府古圖

A Chinese map of Taiwan Fu from the 1696 Taiwan Fu Gazetteer. The islands off the coast make up Lu-er-men harbor. The largest island hosts the old Dutch fort Zeelandia. Also notice the ox-carts pulling passengers in the harbor.

Taiwan Fu

Life in Taiwan Fu is bountiful. The Chinese population has more than doubled since the Dutch left, and now over one hundred thousand people reside on the island, mostly concentrated in this city. Yu finds that only one-thousandth of the island's land is under cultivation. The Dutch found it "a very beautiful and fertile land. It is full of game like deer, pigs, serows [sic], pigeons, partridges, pheasants and the like. And the waters teem with fish."[1] Fertile ground, high rainfall and a year with "more summer than winter" ensure high crop yields, according to the *Taiwan Fu Gazetteer*. Indeed, horticulturist Yu recommends to "just plant and you will certainly profit." Rice kernels grow as big as beans and trees sprout overnight, filled with many leaves. The Gazetteer boasts of Taiwan as a land of plenty, writing of two harvests a year without ever a shortfall, "so people never go hungry...fruit and vegetables grow very well, even in winter; flowers always bloom and the leaves of the trees stay green year round."[2]

Yu studies the Gazetteer and makes his own inquiries and observations. While finding the earth quite fertile, he says it is very dry and victim to the wind "which blows it all about; and the rain leaves it in ditches." The guava fruit grows like a weed however, and Yu finds it "so disgustingly smelly you have to hold your nose." The bananas "make me cold and uncomfortable, sticking to my teeth." Yu does find he likes the coconut and betel nut trees because they stand strait and tall "alone at your door, the leaves dancing in the wind." The thick-peeled red fruit, or watermelon, also makes him happy. It ripens in January and is just as good as Zhangzhou's, but not as good as Quanzhou's.

Such are the reasons why immigrants risk death to come to this Garden of Eden in the sea. Yu says "China's poor just grab a bag and run over." Indeed, the hilly Fujian province has been farmed out, and growing population pressures make land scarce and life unbearable. A bushel of rice costs one hundred strings of cash in a society where the average worker barely makes that much in a month. No one can buy rice, and the merchants' complaints echo louder than the cries of hawkers in the street. Yu says he could "see the hunger in people's faces...the people along the China coast are skinny and pale."

The coastal removal policy, which relocated everything miles inland off the coast and burned the fields, was in place for the twenty years the government needed to pressure the Zhengs into submission. In addition to starving the Zhengs, the coastal removal policy also did a fine job of devastating the land. Some twenty years later, when the people were allowed to move back to their homes they found harvest time past and the scorched land unfarmable. Those that kneaded the land got very low yields.

Stark opposite conditions lay across the strait. Land on the Taiwan frontier was fertile, abundant and just waiting for clearing, a place where "one thousand acres can feed tens of thousands of people and still have food left over," as Yu says. Those that come to labor get a hundred strings of cash a day and "nobody needs to look for money," he says. Butchers hang large gold pieces from their aprons and "if they go and gamble it away it doesn't matter."

Yu finds Taiwan getting richer and China getting poorer. Although he has heard such tales of Taiwan before, not until he comes to the island does he discover why: the absence of monumental wars. The Zheng attack on the

Dutch thirty-six years earlier was waged on the sea and turned into a standoff with little damage to the island's infrastructure. The Qing victory over the Zhengs involved no hostilities against the main island as all warfare took place at Penghu "People have been free from war and have saved money for a long time," Yu writes. Now people grow half a million pounds of sugar cane a year which they sell to Japan and Philippines, and another one hundred thousand pounds of rice, seeds, and beans which they sell all over the world. This gives the island an annual income of some eight hundred thousand taels. To date, the Qing's sixteen-year rule over the island has added around twelve million taels to the state treasury. "Taiwan has so much money coming in and little going out. Compare with China which has a lot of money going out and very little coming in; of course Taiwan will get richer and China poorer," Yu writes.

Of course it hasn't always been this way. Early Taiwan's only residents were headhunting aborigines. The Chinese hardly knew of the island, Yu says. "A great distance stands between Fujian and Taiwan, alienating the previous generations from any contact between them. Although early references describe many barbarian islands in detail, none of them mention Taiwan." Fisherman have come to fish off the coasts for many generations, and although it seems unlikely, some say the great Ming explorer Zheng He stopped in Chikan in the fourteenth century to draw fresh water on his way to distant lands.

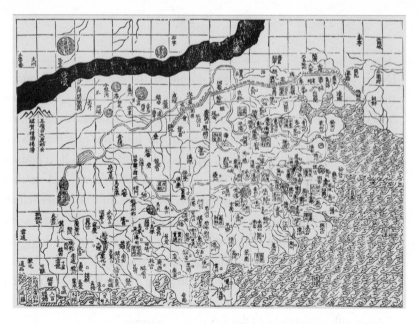

Guang Yu Tu, 1555. One of the first Chinese maps of the world—on which all early western maps of China were based. China is at the very center surrounded by "a myriad of countries."

THE FIRST DISCOVERY

The first documented Chinese landing on the Taiwan island occurred under the Yuan Dynasty (1206-1368). Due to navigational error a Chinese diplomatic envoy on its way to the Ryukyu Islands happened to land on a strange island in the late thirteenth century.[*]

Accordingly, towards the end of the 13th century, the Yuan rulers launched two attacks on Japan, both ending in utter failure, and planned for a third. In order to gain position and avoid repeating the previous bungles,

---

[*] Scholars and governments still argue emotionally over the first Chinese "discovery" of Taiwan. I have weighed all the arguments and found that accounts earlier than the one presented here did not discus Taiwan but other pacific islands, most probably the Ryukyus. For more on this refer to the work of Lai Fu-shun. Specifically, 賴福順, 探索元明時期中國與小琉球國的關係：兼述朱元璋與「兩國論」, in, 中國現代史專題研究報告, 第 22 輯（中華民國史料研究中心, 2001）頁 57-172; 賴福順, 流「中」航線研究（《台灣文獻》卷 54 期 1–2, 2003 年 3 月及 6 月）

they wanted to stage the attack from the south, moving up on Japan from the Ryukyus. In 1291, the emperor called a meeting to plan an attack on Ryukyu. The meeting fell into disarray with two opposing factions "turning red in the face with anger," as the histories say. On the one side stood Yang Xian, leading the charge for increased aggression and full-scale war against anyone who dared challenge the mighty China; and on the other side stood the pacifists, who wanted to avoid hostilities. The meeting adjourned with no decision reached.

However, it did make the talk of Beijing. A Fujian scholar by the name of Wu Zhidou learned of the debate from friends who held positions among the palace officials. Through some channel—though we aren't quite sure how—Wu managed to get a letter into the hands of the emperor, entreating his majesty to let him lead the convoy to Ryukyu. He said he would convince the natives of the island to maintain friendly relations with the Chinese and allow them to stage the attack on Japan from their island. Although the actual letter is gone a poem of Wu's intentions remain:

> *Wu, born on the coast of Fujian.*
>   *He says, "who needs knives and cannon."*
>   *He says, "let me talk and they will comply."*
>   *He says, "if not then I will continue to try."*[3]

The emperor called another meeting, this time with Wu present. Wu said he grew up on the coast and understood the sea and its islands. If the Ryukyuans don't agree to diplomatic negotiations then there is still time to attack, he argued. Unmoved by Wu's arguments Yang Xian continued to press for outright attack. Wu criticized Yang for taking an aggressive position in order to receive rank and historical recognition. The emperor sided with Wu.

In the Spring of 1292 a diplomatic party headed by Yang, Wu, and Ruan Jian, along with a few hundred troops, sailed just a half a day east of Penghu. They saw the long shoreline of an island with high mountains. It is the Ryukyu Island, Yang said. Ruan is not sure. Wu said nothing.

Confident that they had reached their destination, Yang took a landing craft to shore where a large welcoming party had gathered. Seeing the scantily clad dark skinned peoples on shore, Yang remained in the landing craft and sent a general with an interpreter to meet them. The natives did not speak Ryukuan and, not amused by the interpreters' attempts to find a dialect, killed three soldiers. Witnessing the atrocities from the landing craft, Yang quickly returned to the ship.

After three days of anxiety, indecision and vacillation the party returned to Penghu. Yang wanted Wu and Ruan to sign a report that said they arrived at the Ryukyus where the natives refused to negotiate diplomatically. Under the loud and adamant protest of Wu they refused. That night Wu mysteriously disappeared and all on board believed that Yang killed him.[4]

Seventy-five years later, the first emperor of the Ming Dynasty, in utter disgust at Yuan foreign policy, banned aggression on China's eastern neighbors, including Taiwan. "I am afraid subsequent generations will think China thought itself too great and set out to conquer territory just to show off its strength," he said. "In the future, do not wage war against the barbarian countries in the northeast, including Korea, in the east, including Japan, the islands to the east and southeast, including Ryukyu and Taiwan." With this law laid down for his sons and grandsons who will succeed him as emperor, no one paid enough official attention to leave any record of the Taiwan island for the next three hundred years.[5]   ∞

The only known surviving portrait of Qing Navy Admiral Shi Lang. The Qing annexed Taiwan largely due to Shi Lang's lobby.

SHI LANG
AND WHY THE QING OCCUPIED TAIWAN

Although the Qing had plenty of records on Taiwan, not the least of which came from the Zheng occupation, they to wanted little to do with the island. Kangxi ordered his navy commander Shi Lang to Taiwan in the early fall of 1683 to begin depopulating the island and accept the surrender of the Zheng government. The amnesty edict was the standard practice in order to preserve peace and give the appearance of a kind and merciful ruler. Shi Lang noted that the Zhengs "leapt for joy, then kow-towed in the direction of the palaces, giving thanks to the imperial grace that their lives were spared."[6] In preparation to clear out the island, Kangxi brought the Zheng ruler, Zheng Keshuang, to Beijing for house arrest and scattered the some forty thousand Zheng troops near the Russian border. Over half of the Chinese population on Taiwan, most of whom had fled a war stricken China, returned home after twenty years under the oppressive Zheng rule.

The Qing Navy General, Shi Lang, however, had near irrational desires over the island, which put him a few steps in front of official palace policies. When he landed in Taiwan Fu he sent out a proclamation that Taiwan had officially come under Qing rule and spent the next few months touring the island and preparing his argument to change the mind of the emperor and not abandon the land. Late that year, Shi Lang sent long-winded pedantic letters about Taiwan, advising the emperor to keep the island. Though copious, Shi's point is simple, with one overriding argument: security. They painstakingly explored the geographical position of the island, noting that it "protects the four coastal provinces" and its "many harbors and useful bays give strategic hideaway positions."

And if the Qing gave up the naval port, Shi argued, lingering immigrants would group together and join with pirates. "Rebels will rise on Taiwan and terrorize the seas, stealing money and making passage unsafe." Or worse, "the Red Hair people will return to cause trouble in trade and peace." On the tentative proposal to militarily administer Taiwan from bases on Penghu, Shi Lang objected. "Penghu is small and in the middle of the sea. It sits much closer to Taiwan than Jinmen." So adamant the navy general was about colonizing the island that he extrapolated on the richness of the Taiwan soil from which "salt, deerskin, fish, sugar cane, rice and many trees" can support full garrisons. Imperial resources from the mainland needed to govern Taiwan, according to Shi Lang, would be nil.[7]

But there was more. Shi Lang was acutely interested in profit. Not until he had landed and toured the island did he petition zealously to keep it. His previous memorials to the emperor only raised the question of keeping it or not. Shi Lang's hidden agenda was not what Taiwan could offer China but rather what Taiwan could offer him. Upon landing on the island he sought out the English at their trading post, calling them "enemies to the emperor" who "supplied this nest of thieves with ammunition, and sending men to fight too." He then demanded twenty-five hundred taels for himself and five hundred taels for each of his servants, "if they value their lives liberty and company estate." This came on top of the English "present to the value of 3,090 taels" to Shi Lang and two hundred taels to his servant.

Knowing the British were businessmen, not mercenaries, Shi Lang promised in return to petition to the emperor on their behalf to allow them to trade. He subsequently taxed them.[8] Reading between the rice paper lines of Shi Lang's memorials, and chronicling his later exploits, exposes the general in full. He hints at defecting ever so cunningly in his memorials to the emperor. He knows he himself could make use of the harbors and bays, which he lavishly emphasizes could be a hiding place for pirates. The rich natural resources do not fail to tempt him either. And Taiwan's position off the coast of China, suspended in the sea lanes from Japan, Hong Kong and the Philippines, continue to make it the ideal pirate lair.

It seems unlikely that Emperor Kangxi could overlook such facts, and even more unbelievable that the court did not know of Shi Lang's motives. In fact, most of the imperial court sided with their emperor and opposed occupying and governing Taiwan, a place they considered "a pile of rust-brown mud."[9] Even Shi Lang's hometown comrade Li Guangdi, the imperial secretary, who supported Shi Lang's resolve to use force instead of talk against the Zheng, wanted to "empty the land and leave it to the barbarians." Or even better, "rent it to the Dutch for a price and let them administer it."[10] The court was unified in opposition to the occupation of Tai-wan. Court official Wei Yuan voted to set up a military garrison on Penghu. "Taiwan is an orphan island and a likely home for rebels. I don't want it." he said.[11] In their separate reports officials emphasized again and again that Taiwan "drifts in the stream and has never been a part of Chinese territory."[12]

Such arguments should come as no surprise. The Qing had descended from the north, invading China at a break in the Great Wall just above Bei-jing They came on horseback and defeated the lingering Ming armies through their superior riding skills. What would they want with an island? Shi Lang's arguments from the point of the empire's security were unjustified given the size and strength of Kangxi's China, and foreigners were viewed almost as partners, as Li Guangdi testified to. Likewise, the resources on the tiny island paled in comparison to those of the continental mainland. In the end, Kangxi dismissed the place as but a trifle, chastising it like a skin rash: "acquire it and we will have to scratch a lot, lose it and we are probably better off."[13]

It would more than itch if he did acquire it, for he would have to put his trust in the navy (how else would contact with the island ensue), which was composed of sailors who had all deserted the Ming. Kangxi barely trusted Shi Lang to lead the attack on Penghu, not to mention govern Taiwan. His advisors remained adamantly opposed to empowering the navy anyway. As Kangxi put it: "I was warned not to send Shi Lang to lead the campaign against Taiwan because he might rebel if I gave him ships and troops."[14] That was the problem. When Kangxi gave him the title of navy commander and supplied him with ships and troops, his naval power was unmatched and in many ways unchecked. In the end he did send Shi Lang because "unless you are sent to Taiwan it will never be pacified."[15] Even so, doubts remained.

In January 1684, court officials entrusted to decide on the Taiwan question traveled to Fujian to meet with Shi Lang. They concluded almost too readily and presented the emperor with an affirmative answer to "keep the land stretching for thousands of miles and occupied by ten thousand people." The navy general's influence is unmistakable. The memorial to the emperor recommending to keep Taiwan details all of Shi Lang's arguments on security as well as presents his proposals on how to staff garrisons and post officials.

Kangxi, ever wary, rejected the court's proposal and sent them back to discuss it again. After only six days they returned with the same suggestion to keep Taiwan. Kangxi dismissed them and mulled on the problem. Stewing it like a vat of oil and water he contradicted his own thinking and anybody that tried to agree or disagree with him. When his secretary, seemingly siding with him, advised against retaining the island, Kangxi bursts out, "Oh, and I won't keep all of the thirteen provinces either!?"

Then, four months later, without any warning, Kangxi had enough of indecisiveness and gave his consent to occupy Taiwan. On May 27, 1684, almost a year after the Zheng surrender, he issued a imperial edict stating that for the first time in history "Taiwan leaves the outside seas and comes under [Chinese] jurisdiction."[16] New on the Chinese map.[17]   ❧

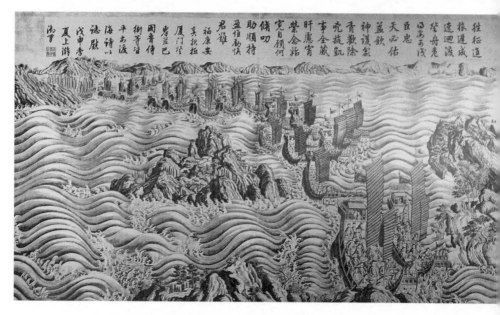

The Qing Navy landing on Taiwan to put down a rebellion. From Pictures on the Pacification of Taiwan, *1789.*

SHI LANG AND GOVERNING TAIWAN

E ven after making the momentous decision, Kangxi wanted little to do with what he called "that desolate place." He dumped policymaking on his court officials who bickered about it among themselves constantly, and when they finally suggested something for his approval the emperor always contradicted them. At one point he cried that the proposal to rotate officials every three years was stupid and "we can't just move people around all the time!"[18] In the end the county magistrate and military garrisons stationed in Taiwan were rotated every three years then later reduced to one. Or when officials tried to persuade the emperor to open up and cultivate land on Taiwan as it "will bring much profit, and promises to be good for the entire social order on the island," Kangxi refused: "To open Taiwan and encourage people to immigrate is to sacrifice our ears for our eyes. When Fujian is no longer poor and burdened with conflict then we can talk about Taiwan."[19] End of conversation, the frontier state does not concern us. Rule it like the Zhengs did and the Dutch before them.

After Kangxi died and passed the throne to his heirs who were more attentive to the island, the question of how to administer Taiwan continued to torment the Qing for the duration of their rule. It did make the Qing very adept at dragging out debates, the acute reality of failing to come to any conclusion about how to govern Taiwan made a mess of social order. Settlers pushed to open up the frontier, and officials could not decide if they approved or not. Initially they disapproved, as the government had not made Taiwan a province and hoped to simply remove or contain the immigrants living there. But more snuck across the strait and pushed beyond controlled areas anyway, forcing the court into more quarrels and confusion. The process of governing played out like an absurd drama of try and fail. Indeed, the question of how to rule Taiwan haunted the Qing court for the next two hundred years, in which the issues of immigration, taxes and land reclamation passed, got reversed, then passed again all in the name of stability and Qing rule, but all failing as rebellion constantly plagued the island.

Crouching under the early debates was Shi Lang, the sly Navy general whose keen sense of smell propelled him ahead of the Qing bureaucracy, forcing officials to stop debating and begin following the trends his lead made. When he landed on the main Taiwan island in 1683, Shi Lang seized all of the land held under Zheng government control, taking a sizeable chunk of 7,500 jia (or about 18,000 acres) for himself and dividing up the rest among his loyal troops. Shi Lang's cut was 40 percent of the total registered land on Taiwan, while his first officer got 2,000 jia, or about 10 percent. Total land registered with the government came out to 18,000 jia, but interestingly enough, all the land seized by Shi Lang and his troops went unregistered—for tax purposes. Including the military's share, estimates put total cultivatable land in Taiwan at the time at 30,000 jia. This still gave Shi Lang a quarter of the island for himself, and left almost half in military hands.[20]

As the Qing navy admiral on Xiamen, Shi could not very well administer all this land himself, nor did he want to. Shi Lang sent over relatives and friends from Fujian to collect taxes and rent out the land to farmers willing to cultivate. From the rent, the Shi relatives would pay the taxes. The renter often paid out a percentage of his yield to the owner as rent and the owner paid half of that amount in taxes.[21] The tenant never paid taxes, only rent on his harvest. This enabled tenants to amass enough wealth to split up the land into plots and rent out the plots to poorer farmers. In this way, the main landlord received 10 percent of the yield from the secondary landlord, who usually received 30-50 percent from his tenant.[22] This could seep down into three or four landlord-like-middlemen creating, as the saying went, "one plot of land with three masters." The Zhejiang-Fujian governor-general Gao Qizhou summed up the whole process: "to open up new areas, settlers were called in. But military officers, from the first commander Shi Lang on down, all claimed land. Local civil and military officials established official estates, and powerful families arbitrarily seized land for reclamation, called in tenants, and collected rents. Later on, tenants themselves called in tenants and with transfers back and forth, layer by layer, ownership is concealed."[23] In this way, Shi Lang's land seizures directly defined the structure of class relations that would develop on the new frontier, where only 30-40 percent of owners cultivated the land themselves, and the rest of the population toiled and rebelled.[24]

The gazetteers in 1732 justified such practices because "it's in accordance with village custom."[25] But such a system did not come without its problems. Most pressing were the complaints about Shi Lang. The British in their dealing with Shi Lang recorded that "now the Chinese, but too late, begin to repent and to be grievously afraid when they see him gape daily for large bribes."[26] In a letter straight to the emperor, Xu Langbin, an official stationed on Penghu, called Shi Lang a "cheap and petty general who requests too much and gives nothing." He detailed how all the fishermen were exploited by his greed and all the immigrants crossing the sea lie at his mercy.[27] Indeed, Shi's land seizures were draconian and cheated people out of their land. Ji Lingguang, an official on Taiwan, related that "Shi steals the land from the people then rents it back to them. The people are bad off. Everyday they cry in anguish."[28] ❦

Yu does not find things to be so bad in Taiwan Fu. But he is only here as a visitor on an official assignment to collect sulfur. He has not come to Taiwan to live, and Taiwan Fu is not even his final destination. Yu must still travel for weeks up the coast of the island to the far north. Still, that does not stop the adventurer from resting and observing the settlement on the Qing's new frontier.

Set on the southwestern coast of the island, Yu notes that Taiwan Fu is flush with Chinese characteristics yet also has its own personality. The roads are reminiscent of Beijing but somewhat simpler. They are divided into three sections with the center for carts and the sides filled with stalls. The women on Taiwan, though few in number, do not bind their feet as the mainland customs dictate. "There is nothing good to look at below the skirt's hemline," Yu muses. The immigrants use foreign money, which are long oval shaped coins engraved with a Dutch emblem. This "Red Haired Barbarian money" is the only form of currency the locals will accept. Yu is amused to find the stall keepers shake their heads when he tries to use Qing coins.

The city still lacks infrastructure. Due to the journey across the sea, the Qing have not imported many horses to the island. The ten thousand troops stationed on the island have less than one thousand horses among them. Likewise, the scarcity of rocks in the area and the impracticality of bringing them across the strait has left Taiwan Fu without a stone wall; only bamboo stakes attempt to protect the city from attack, leaving the capital of Taiwan vulnerable in times of war. The Taiwan administration has planned to build a wall many times, but because the rock quarries lie far inland with no water access, officials have given up.

Yu learns as much and subsequently devises an intricate plan to plant three levels of bamboo around the city. He notes that Taiwan's bamboo grows very close together"so close that a hair cannot fit between the stalks...this is more solid than rocks and doesn't need to be built, just let it grow." He suggests requiring every household to plant stalks so that "within a few months Taiwan Fu will be as hard as steel."[29] Perhaps, but no one is listening to Yu; it will take another one hundred years and a massive siege on Taiwan Fu before the government constructs a perimeter wall—made from stone.

Even though the Zheng rebels have been conquered and the straggling armies left on Taiwan repatriated to the frigid borders of northern China, rebellion remains a threat. As Yu puts it, "Taiwanese like to rebel." Yu notes that every year someone rises up, claims themselves as king or some other high official and tries to sack the capital. "Although they die at the clubs of officials, more and more people continue to rebel," he writes. Most often the disgruntled immigrants from Zhangzhou lash out at fellow settlers from Quanzhou. Water and land rights often act as the catalyst. If the rebellion gains ground, people will mobilize and with enough strength, move on Taiwan Fu. Yu says they are not bad people, but rather are attempting to emulate the Zheng resistance. They hope to surrender and secure a position as an official. If the rebellion succeeds you become emperor, if it fails you surrender and become an official. So "everyone flies like birds to rebel," Yu writes.

Yu gets an audience with captured rebels. He asks them why they rebelled.

"I am not rebelling," they say.

"You lie, you have banners and dynasty names," he counters.

"I hope to surrender and get a government rank," they say.

Yu explains that the times since the Zhengs have changed, and now that Taiwan has been pacified the Qing the government will not give out ranks to rebels. "Every rebellion goes on a case by case basis," he says.

Captured rebels will receive the "lingering death," also known as "death by a thousand cuts," the most severe penalty for plotting against the dynasty.

Laws in Taiwan Fu have always been strict. The Dutch erected gallows in Chikan and put them to good use on ill-behaved Chinese and aborigines alike. The Zhengs had policies of no forgiveness for rape or stealing. "To take as much as a stalk of bamboo would result in decapitation," contemporaries say. Such stringent rules have bred habits into the locals. They don't pick up anything left out on the street that does not belong to them, in fact people leave things out and no one steals them.

Yu has been in Taiwan Fu for over a month now. He has spent 980 taels on sulfur extracting supplies, including oil and pots to burn sulfur, a ladle to move sulfur into the big pot, and small wooden boxes to store the sulfur. He has also bought, cloth to trade with aborigines, sugar to give to workers as an antioxidant, a shovel to dig pits, knives, axes and a sickle to cut wood and grass, a big wooden box to hold water, scales and rulers "to measure things", and beans, smokes, bowls and chopsticks for one hundred people. He purchases a ship to carry everything, but can only pack in seven-tenths of the supplies, so he buys another ship for only half the price of the first to stuff the rest into.

All is set. Yu is excited to explore this land "no one knows," but that afternoon, as he prepares to board the ship, the warnings come. The Taiwan Fu magistrate and general tell him not to go: "Have you not heard of Jilong and Danshui? The water and rocks there are very evil. People get sick and die!" They tell Yu that servants who know of the north will not even go when ordered. "They scream as if they were being sent to hell," the magistrate says. Even the coast guard feel themselves lucky if they make it back safely from their periodic patrols to the north. "If these strong fit men have such fears, what of you?" The two officials recommend Yu send his servants while he remains in Taiwan Fu. A friend from Fengshan County relates the tale of an army general who led one hundred troops into an area near Lower Danshui to put down a rebellion. "Within two months they were all dead," he cries. "If Lower Danshui is like this, Jilong and Danshui will be even worse!" Another official traveled north with four of his friends, the friend says, and "only their corpses returned."

The tales do not stop, and with them the horror stories mount. In the north is Jilong, or "Chicken Cage," sitting on the eastern side of the northern tip of the island. Its small round hills dotting the coastline rise out of the water with pointy caps, making them appear like traditional cages to trap chickens. Black water runs by the coast here, which won't even support vegetation, and which has been known to sink ships.[30] The ocean runs to the east here with great ferocity as if it is being sucked down a funnel. Contemporary tales say that ships get pulled to the end of the earth and cannot return. Yet these are only myths that no one knows for sure. Ships that have traveled east never return, flat earth tales instill sailors with fear and now no one dares venture to the east coast. This has resulted in a situation where the west doesn't know the east and the east doesn't know the west.

The Spanish lost four to five ships in half a year in Jilong. "Everyday there are many who sail out but shipments are lost due to the rough sea coast," wrote Fr. Jacinto Esquivel.[31] His comrade in conversion, Fr. Martinez, drowned trying to sail out of Danshui in 1629 to report the Spanish victory over the Dutch in the north. And then, when the Dutch returned to avenge their losses some twenty years later, their ship smashed against the harbor rocks.

Yu listens intently to the tales of danger. They seem to excite him. "If I am born I will die. What can water and dirt do to me?!" He tells his friends that he must watch the workers already organized for the trip, as well as the hundreds of aborigines solicited to help. "The place I am going is near the savages. If I don't go forth and control them we might have problems."

Seeing that Yu will not deviate from his plan to travel to the north, his friends give him antidotes to guard against snake venom and other animal poisons, and medicines to fend off dysentery and other diseases stalking travelers in the northern forests. They tell him three times to take care.

Again, as Yu prepares to sail, an official named Gu who comes from the same town in Jiangnan as Yu, tells him not to travel by boat along the Taiwan coast. "Those who are wise do not do what you are doing," he warns Yu. "You should flee from danger and stay near safety." Gu has been posted in Taiwan for many years and knows the dangers of the island. He has heard many stories of coastal wrecks and informs Yu that "ocean going ships do not fear the open sea but they will not go near the cliffs. They do not fear deep water but avoid shallow harbors. The Taiwan coast is uncharted and if you hit coral you will definitely sink, it will punch a hole in your ship and you will face defeat. From here to Jilong heavy winds will chase you and no safe harbors will offer their protection for you to anchor. It is much more dangerous than the open ocean."

Yu listens but is stubborn in his resolve and will not sacrifice his mission due to these speculative dangers. Later he will write that "if the journey is not dangerous then it is not exciting; if it does not involve difficulty then I will not enjoy it."[32] So when Gu proposes to travel by the land route instead, Yu is intrigued. Gu even offers to accompany Yu. "If you want me to go with you and will not go by land then I will refuse." Yu accepts Gu's suggestion and accepts his offer to travel together overland. However, he will still send his two ships with supplies by water. "Wang likes the convenience of the ship. I cannot change his mind," Yu says.

There are two types of savages, the cooked and the raw. The raw savages live in holes in the ground and they drink blood and eat hair. They are especially fierce and strong. They often come out to steal things, burn houses and kill people. Then they return to their nests so there is no way to catch them. When they kill they take the head and when they return they cook it. They strip the skull and sprinkle it with powder, setting it before their door. The one from the same tribe who has the most skulls is the hero. The cooked savages fear them and do not dare enter their territory.

YU YONGHE

[One tribe] assailed the others very bravely, first with assegais and thereafter with shields and swords. They hacked each other into a hodgepodge with astonishing courage.

GERRIT FREDERICKSZ DE WITT, DUTCH COMMANDER

PART 4

The Aborigines,
Cooked

Landtag auf der Insul Formosa.

A meeting of the aborigine tribes with Dutch administrators at Chikan. In 1650, 350 aborigine tribes submitted to Dutch authority and traveled to the Dutch castle to show their subservience.

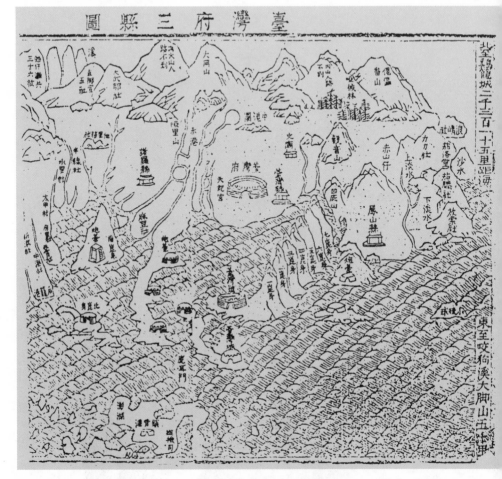

Taiwan Fu and the three counties, from right to left, Fengshan, Taiwan, and Zhuluo. From the 1684 Taiwan Gazetteer.

The Aborigines, Cooked

MAY 26

ON THE ROAD OUT OF TAIWAN FU

Yu and Gu ride in ox pulled carts out of Taiwan Fu. They are accompanied by fifty-five troops, servants, aborigines and workers.

It is the seventh day of the fourth month in the thirty-sixth year of the Kangxi reign.

As the party moves north they pass through three aborigine villages where Yu gets his first close up look at the living environments of the aborigines. "They are no worse than the homes in China," he says. Then turning to Gu asks, "Who says the aborigines are dirty and inferior? You really can't believe what others tell you."

Because these villages are within the immediate vicinity of Taiwan Fu, they are the most assimilated. Their homes are kept spotlessly clean and made from high quality wood. The Dutch had particular interest in the houses here as well, noting with awe that they are "so obscure and dark that on a bright afternoon you cannot recognize each other except from very close by, they try to darken their houses even more in daylight by closing their doors, so they seem to live in a stuffy, dark cellar."[1]

The Qing have continued efforts to Sinicize these villages by allowing them to forgo taxes if the village children receive a formal Chinese education. Their close proximity to Taiwan Fu allows them to send their children into the city to study. Gu calls them "quite civilized," and says that "these villages all cultivate their fields and save the profits. They are fairly rich. And because they are close to the capital they observe people's manners." The village of Ou Wang lies near the coast, situated in a main traffic artery. For this reason, Gu says, it has more money than the other three. "Too bad we do not have the opportunity to go see it, for after this area the villages become worse and worse."

In Madou Village they change carts and get fresh oxen to pull them. Yu sees some of the males and females of the villages with uncut hair and wearing only skirts "just like the savages-of-old." Yu doesn't eat with the local savages, instead he lets a local official cook lunch for him.

As dark settles, they arrive in Jia-li-xing, about 25 kilometers southwest from their destination. "The savages don't understand what we are saying!" Yu cries. "They see me talking with another official and assume that I am going in the same direction."

There are no beds and Yu does not know where to sleep. He goes to a village official's house to find a bed.

MAY 27

ON THE ROAD NORTHWARDS

Yu has lost a day. By the time the party reaches Dao-luo-guo, their destination village of yesterday, it is already dark. A light wind blows out of the south and Yu thinks of Wang sailing north. "In no time he can travel thousands of miles" he laments. Yu fears that Wang will arrive in Danshui long before him, so he feels he must make better time on the road. Yu does not stop to rest but pushes forward, crossing the raging Bazhang Creek. By morning they have reached Zhuluo. The sun is up but everyone is tired. They must stop and rest.

Yu rides an ox-driven cart commanded by an aborigine. He has spent two days and two nights on the cart. Although he tries to sleep he cannot. Every time the road narrows and they pull close to a steep cliff "it scares me wide awake."

Yu studies the tattoos on the aborigine driving his cart. The man's back has a giant bird with its wings stretched out. Across his shoulders and stomach are dark diagonal lines. Human heads stare at Yu from the driver's biceps. "Those on his neck are even more terrifying," Yu observes. His forearms have large metal bracelets stacked up to the elbows, while from his ears hang heavy rings, stretching the lobes to abnormal proportions. Indeed, "the males like big ears," Yu writes. They use rings to stretch them and continue to insert larger and larger pieces of bamboo shoots into the hole until the ear expands to shoulder or even chest level.

Yu sees many tattoos on the bodies of the aborigine males: birds, tigers, leopards, fishnets, "so many it's hard to explain them all." They wear shells as necklaces, often very many of them in different styles. "Its very strange," he remarks. Yu tells us the aborigines have a rich tradition of shaving their body hair. They shave in five places, though Yu does not say where.

That night Yu stays in Caili Village.

MAY 29

ON THE ROAD NORTHWARDS

Yu's party crosses two rivers, one of them is almost two kilometers wide. The smooth rocks allow them to walk across easily and Yu wonders if this is what they call "steel plate sand." He cannot see it unless he reaches down into the water to grab the rocks in his hands. The water is black from the mountain runoffs, carrying the hills' fertile black dirt down and out to sea.

In the next six kilometers they cross many more rivers. Some are deep and move swiftly, making it hard to wade through. At one crossing, the oxen disappear under the water, only their noses visible, gasping for air. Ten aborigines grab a hold of the wheels of the cart in an attempt to prevent it from getting swept away. In the process everyone is sucked under. In fact, they are lucky. As soon as the party has crossed and rests safely on the opposite shore it begins to rain, sending a flash flood between the banks.

Yu observes the different aborigines now accompanying him. These peoples have even more tattoos and their "ears are the size of bowls." They braid their hair and coil it on the top of their head and tie it up with tree vines. Bugs sometimes stick to the vine and crawl around their heads, inciting derogatory remarks about cleanliness from their Chinese conquerors. The young girls use oil to make two ponytails. Yu thinks it good looking. The wind ruffles the three chicken feathers perched in their hair. He sees three girls breaking grain on stone millets and hesitantly notes his first attraction to the aborigine women. "One is very pretty but wears no clothes. They all think it very natural."

Yu is confused about his feelings towards aborigine women. He finds some of the younger ones very pretty but "they put deer oil in their hair, which smells just horrendous and one can't even get near them." He notes with fascination that aborigine sex life and marriages are maternal-based and void of matchmakers. When the female matures her parents give her a private room. At night young men come to see her and play a nose pipe. If the woman sings with the suitor then he can enter and "get nasty," as Yu says. "After the nasty he can leave." *

The Dutch explorers also lost themselves in joyous description of these practices. Reverend Georgius Candidius explained that after the act the man "must rise and slink away without speaking a word (like the fox from the henhouse) and he is not allowed to come back to the house during the day."[2] They explained that after experimenting for a time the woman will choose a man she likes, expressed by holding hands with him. Only then will she marry him. The next day, she takes him to meet her parents. The male extracts his two front teeth and gives them to her. She in turn pulls her two

---

* Yu uses the character luan 亂 to refer to the act of sex.

front teeth to give to him. The man comes and lives in the woman's home. This maternal-based society leaves no line of descendants, for the son cannot stay at home. The aborigines have no surname.

Yu arrives at village of Da-wu-jun for the night.

MAY 30

BANXIAN VILLAGE

Yu walks 15 kilometers today to Banxian Village. They have not traveled far but Yu is cheered by the hospitality at this village. A local cries out to him to "stop and rest...the oxcarts have a hard time coming over the rock road, not to mention walking!"

Before he sleeps, Yu notes that "from Zhuluo to here all the aborigine women have beautiful white skin. They are all very pretty."

Yu has almost experimented with his own sexual desires towards the aborigine women, once expressing attraction to another aborigine man's wife. He notes that the man did not get angry but in turn felt "prideful that he has such a pretty wife that a Chinese will like."

Indeed, Dutch explorer Elie Ripon wrote that when complaining to his host that he could not sleep well without a mattress, the latter "replied that he would find me a woman to serve as a mattress. I answered that I was not used to such kind of mattress."[3] Nor were fellow explorers Pessaert and Constant, who traveled to a neighboring village and noted that "they do not seem to be very jealous about their wives, nor do they deem the act of procreation improper: because it happened to us, being there, that a man after having made love to his wench (spoken with reverence) in a natural way (and that in our presence), took her by the hand and led her to us, to do the same with her and replace him in his labor; this we refused on the grounds of being an un-Christian act, which astonished them."[4] But, Yu says, if another aborigine tries to make advances on his wife, the husband will "use the bow and arrow to kill him, and never blame the woman."

MAY 31

CENTRAL TAIWAN

Yu's fantasies with aborigine women have deteriorated. "It's a different world beyond Banxian. The aborigines begin to look ugly and savage."

An unusual amount of rocks litter the path throwing the cart in every which way as it bumps along. They cross so many rivers that Yu cannot record them all.

JUNE 1

SHALU, CENTRAL TAIWAN

They cross a large swollen river into Shalu. The rain that has just let up has left them wet. They stop at an aborigine village to find a place to rest. The houses here stand on stilts with a short flight of stairs up to an open doorway. Yu is pleased that his sleeping mat is beside an open window.

Dutch troops taking action against rioting Chinese in Zhangjou, Fujian in 1622.
By Francois Valentyn.

THE DUTCH AS COLONIZERS

Yu has been on the road for only five days but he has already spent some time with the aborigines of the south. These are the tribes that are tame. Yu says that if these aborigines kill people now it is not to rebel but because they drink liquor and get carried away in their strength competitions. "Before the cup has left one's hand a knife is already at the other's throat," Yu says. When they get angry without intoxication they just glare, Yu says, but with a bit of liquor they will attack. "Afterwards they forget all about the incident."

When the Dutch first arrived, however, the southern aborigines were out for heads. In fact, tribes all over the island lived in a primitive state of nature, so to say, in which they constantly went to war with each other, collecting heads and mounting the skulls before their doors. As Governor Martinus Sonck noted in 1625, "they are embroiled in interactive wars most of the time and the bravest man in war enjoys the most authority."[5] The Dutch had plenty of opportunities to observe these wars in which the natives "hacked each other into a hodgepodge with astonishing courage."[6] Tribal warfare consisted of waiting until night and sneaking up on slumbering victims of another tribe. "When they find someone, be they old or young, woman or man, they kill that person without any niceties, chop off the head, hands and feet, sometimes even take the whole body cut into pieces with them," the Reverend Georgius Candidius recorded. This dismembering of victims was a common practice of the aborigines. Candidius said that "they hold these heads, hair, arms, legs or parts of the bones in great esteem and high value, just like we value silver, gold, pearls or any precious stone. When a house is on fire they will save this first."[7] On the island of Xiao Liuqiu, off the coast of southern Taiwan, Dutch Commander Claes Bruyn noted that tribes from the mainland "sometimes come to the island unexpectedly in the night, as is their habit, in a small vessel, to raid not the whole island but just to burgle an isolated house like thieves, without being seen, beating to death every soul they come across—even the infants—taking the heads, arms, feet and hair."[8]

The aborigines did not exhibit better behavior for the colonizers or immigrants, who referred to them as "a disorderly, fierce, malicious, lazy, and greedy people." Both Dutch and Chinese often found themselves at the receiving end of truculent beatings while out fetching water or on a jaunt through the woods. The natives burnt down fields and villages, and even Chinese, who were respected among the aborigines because they traded salt, could get slaughtered when out on a merchant run. The culprits: "strange or unknown natives who wander throughout the whole country."[9] Governor Sonck said that "they set fire to everything and are an irrational people."[10]

The worst massacre came in 1629 as the Dutch were still settling into their new kingdom and trying to open up trade routes. Accordingly, Governor Putmans sent an expedition of sixty-three men out to Madou to find a Chinese pirate. The villagers, providing gracious cooperation, told the Europeans that the pirate had not come their way and gave them a wonderful meal. As was customary practice, the villagers accompanied the Dutch on their return route offering to carry them across a large river; first their firearms then their persons. With no reason to be suspicious, the soldiers accepted, only to have an ambush of aborigines jump out of the bushes and kill them "in a most brutal way" as soon as the soldiers were separated from their weapons. Only a Chinese interpreter and a black slave escaped.

Less than three months later, a similar debacle took place on a northern river where Madou villagers slaughtered fifty-two soldiers and officers.[11]

Part of the problem in bringing the aborigines under colonial control was the lack of subservience to any authority figure. Tribal social structure made each member the exact equal of the other. Village leaders enjoyed no more privilege than anyone else, and even if each village had more than one leader, each leader enjoyed no greater privilege than the rest of the village. "Not like Guangdong or Yunnan where village chiefs can collect taxes, raise an army and kill people," as a contemporary Chinese official noted.[12] The aborigines on Taiwan had no aspirations to rise to these synthetic hierarchical levels, rather, as a Dutch commander said, "they are all satisfied with being equal." The aborigines did not even have words for master or servant in their language, though they did honor bravery in war, where the boldest and most courageous in battle gains the larger following.[13]

Yet bravery was not something the Dutch had to offer. The ministers trying to discipline aborigines in Christian ways could not control them, discovering that "should I lead someone today, tomorrow he will be gone into the fields, and sometimes does not come home again within the month. When there are a few who listen to me tractably, the moment they come into contact with a certain group of people that does not want to listen to me, they destroy it and spoil in one hour more than I have built up in ten."[14]

The Dutch aimed to, as Governor Sonck put it, "bring the inhabitants of this island under the authority of the High and Mighty States General of the United Netherlands."[15] So the pacification efforts began, in which, as one Chinese official put it, "the Dutch took no mercy upon the savages."[16] Reverend Robertus Junius cried, "Oh, if only it should please God that we would gain victory over these people, that would bring so many good results with it, not only a solid foundation for this building but also an excellent instrument to the salvation of these surrounding villages among whom we have come to be held in low esteem."[17]

In 1635, the first major offensive was launched against Madou, the village responsible for the murder of Dutch subjects. It suffered from smallpox at the time and half of its fighters had already died. "Time seems ripe for the destruction or conquest of the village of Madou," Governor Hans Putmans mused.[18] In November that year, Putmans led five hundred European soldiers into Madou killing twenty-six men, women and children; their aborigine abettors taking their victims' body parts with them. As Putmans latter said of the triumph: "We had everything burnt down by the next day (except those trees that did not catch fire) as a means of punishment and revenge for the vile murder committed on our people six and a half years before."

The next month they attacked Xinhua, sending the villagers running to the hills as they razed the entire village, leaving behind only a mound of smoldering ash. With that, Putmans announced that the Dutch authority now expanded to one and a half days walk to the north, south and east of Chikan. "Thus our name, power and authority among these impudent pagans and surrounding villages will be magnified and strengthened now they have seen what we are able to accomplish."[19] Indeed, fifty-seven villages fell in line, subservient to the Dutch. Within ten years and after three major campaigns, the Dutch had brought the whole island under their control so that fifty years later even the anti-Red Hair Barbarian *Taiwan Fu Gazetteer* would note that "the savages wrote red-hair characters and did math."[20]

It was a massive effort, and although some would say it eventually brought about their own downfall—as well as the destruction of the aborigine tribes—the Dutch pacification efforts laid the foundations for growth and development on Taiwan. When the Dutch first arrived on the main Taiwan island in 1623 they found less than 1,500 Chinese immigrants settled there. Although the boat ride across the strait proved a great obstacle and the infamous Black Ditch kept many from trying in the early days, the fierce aborigines tribes, who were constantly at war with each other over the prized body parts, did not allow ill-equipped Chinese settlers to last long even if they did make it to the island. The aborigines seized any opportunity to attack and kill unsuspecting settlers.

Drawing water was the usual opportunity for aborigine ambush. Tales tell that settlers needed to go out armed, or if they didn't they would come back short a few men after a trip to the river. As Reverend Candidius put it, "they do not live in peace and good harmony with one another, but are continuously at war, one village against the other."[21] Elie Ripon, at the head of the first Dutch exploration party in 1623, found himself at the seat of one of these wars when he landed with his men. The aborigines came, he writes, "heavily armed, three or four hundred in all, armed with cutlasses, shields, javelins, lances, bows and arrows."[22] In the battle that followed the Dutch lost three men, but were able to kill some ninety aborigines under the fire-power of five of their muskets.

The Dutch put their superior weaponry to use against the natives right from the start. Ripon says the aborigines would perform rituals before setting out to war "crying and shouting like madmen." Whereas the Dutch would aptly "hand them a match." Ripon says "the natives called the muskets matches because in the forest they saw that I ignited them with a flint, and looking at them from the woods they called the cannons candlesticks, because they gave so much light." He relates the grand tale of when the natives crept close to the fortress and tried to set the bamboo stockade alight. "When one man tried to set the wall afire, a watchman handed him a match' with his musket and shot him dead. The cannons were fired into the dark where the other assailants were thought to be waiting. Not until the next morning the Dutch could see close to their fortress a lot of spilt blood and even limbs and weapons of wounded warriors who had been pulled away by their comrades in the dark."[23]

With this superior weaponry, the Dutch were able to tip the balance of power in their favor, subduing the savages and securing safe areas. Just two years after the Dutch landing, Governor-General Pieter de Carpentier records that "the influx of Chinese has multiplied greatly."[24] He notes that the Taiwan island had accumulated around two thousand Chinese immigrants, mostly fishermen.[25] The European colonizers further encouraged Chinese immigration to Taiwan in order to grow crops and raise a colony. Within the next forty years the Chinese population would grow exponentially. 1640: population 4,995. 1650: population 15,000. 1661: population 35,000.[26] By the time the Dutch left in 1662, the highest estimates put the population at 50,000 Chinese immigrants.[27]   ↻

Robertus Junius arrived in Taiwan in 1628 as the second Dutch missionary to the island. The text around the portrait reads, "Active on Formosa for 14 years, then returned to Delft (Netherlands) for 7 years, now preaching in Amsterdam. Age 48."

Han Chinese settlers in Taiwan. From a Dutch engraving,
published in 1667.

THE ZHENGS AS COLONIZERS

When Zheng Chenggong robbed the Dutch of their hard won colonial conquest, inheriting a growing Chinese population, his administrators moved to make the aborigine tribes as Chinese as possible. The wake of the Dutch ships hadn't even settled before Zheng got to work. In 1662, a Zheng official remarked that the aborigines exhibit "barbarian behavior and are very wasteful. We must send people to instruct them."[28] The Zheng decision makers bickered and stalled, complaining that the whole island had not been explored, the aborigines were not yet pacified, and many places remained very poor. "If we don't educate and civilize people are they any different from animals?" asked Zheng advisor Chen Yunghua.[29]

It almost came as a threat to Zheng Jing who, as a Chinese born ruler, had that innate aversion to barbarians and animal subjects. So began the slow and often staggered process of the Sinicization of Taiwan with Chen Yunghua in command. Within two years officials went into the villages and by 1665 they had set up schools. Chen taught people how to make clay shingles for the roofs of their houses, and used the shingles on a Confucian temple in Taiwan Fu in 1666.

Under Chen, an official two-tier examination system began, in which subjects, by the passing of two tests, could become an official. These exams were held in direct connection with the series of schools established in administered areas, and as an incentive to attend, the government allowed students to be exempt from labor service. The *Taiwan Fu Gazetteer* noted that under Zheng rule, "the younger generation knows they should study the classics and learn to read."[30] Zheng managed this under a rule more strict than the Dutch. They would slaughter the aborigines, leaving not even their children to survive, burning their houses and fields to ash. ೞ

Savages'houses like the nests of ants,

 low thatched roofs without a boon.

The mist blowing in the windows

 and bringing the sea into the room.

I escape the rain leaving footprints.

 It drenches the beds where we stoop.

The river rises and we must stop

 stuck like chickens in a coop.

YU YONGHE

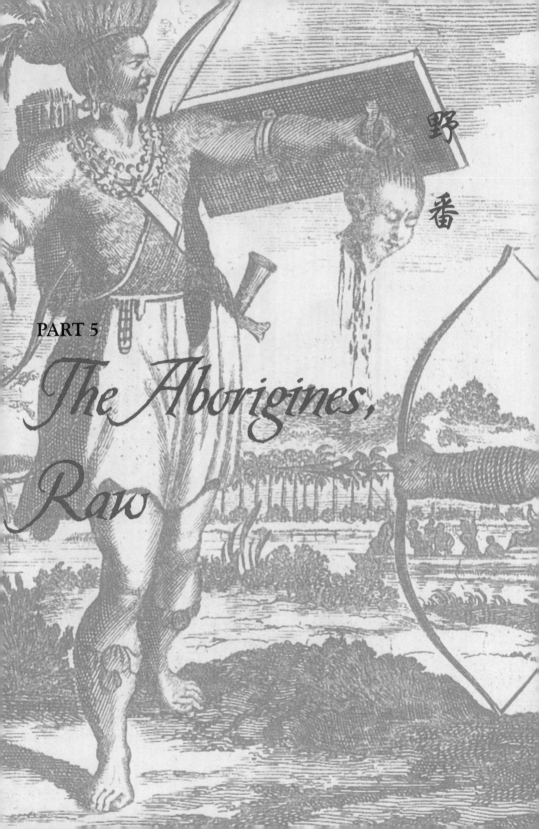

野

番

PART 5

The Aborigines,
Raw

M. Balen delin.

H. F. Diamaer fec. 1726.

An aborigine funeral, by Francis Valentyn, 1724-1726.

Dutch engraving of headhunting aborigines.

The Aborigines, Raw

The rains have come again, and they come in torrents. The dirt path has turned to mud and the rivers rage. Yu and his party cannot press ahead, they cannot even leave their borrowed huts.

Just past noon the rain eases and the sound of the ocean howling creeps inland to haunt the travelers all night. The villagers say that when the ocean cries like this it will continue to rain mercilessly.

JUNE 3

SHALU

The villagers are right. It rains ceaselessly for two days and two nights, falling from the heavens in a torrential downpour. The river ahead is swollen with runoff water gushing angrily out of the hills. Yu does not dare cross, he does not even dare to explore the village.

Every year the spring unloads buckets of water on the island, and every fall and winter the rain falls for months on end. The summers usually only bring afternoon thundershowers, which roll in and cool a land oppressed by the blazing sun before quickly taking their leave. The only thing one can be certain about in the Taiwan climate is heat and humidity. Yu's indoctrination has begun and he writes that "every season is summer, it is hot, humid, and miserably stuffy."[1] Commodore Pickering, a nineteenth-century British adventurer, also came to intimately know the island's weather, writing of a "sun oppressive in its power and the air filled with dust...a climate rendered miserable in the winter months and sugar season by myriads of flies and fleas."[2]

JUNE 5
SHALU

The rain has stopped and the thick fog finally begins to lift. Yu's bed faces the mountains but the heavy rains and fog have blocked them from view. "Fog so thick it is like rain," Yu says. Now, as the sky begins to clear, he has full view of the central mountain range and foothills. "I am over-joyed!" he cries.

The mountain Yu looks at, and which has filled him with immense excitement, is "raw aborigine" territory. The raw aborigines (as opposed to the cooked aborigines) live in the mountains and do not submit to Qing control. "The savages in the mountains don't come out to communicate with the outside world, and the outside world does not go in," the villagers say. The cooked aborigines live on the plains, they pay taxes and trade with the Chinese. The Qing have three conditions that must be met in order for an aborigine to be considered cooked:

1. They must work in the act of carrying letters, carrying supplies, pulling carts, building houses and obeying government orders.
2. Their sons must go to school and receive proper education.
3. They must pay taxes.[3]

1. Zheng Chenggong ordering Dutch missionary Hambrook to return to the Dutch castle and demand the Dutch to surrender. When Hambrook came back with a negative answer, Zheng supposedly killed him. Although this painting is from 1905, it is one of the only Western depictions of Zheng.

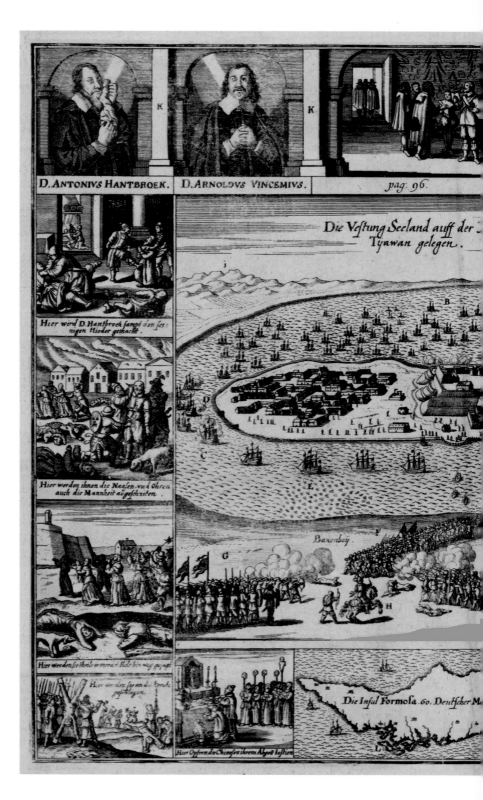

D. ANTONIVS HANTBROEK.   D. ARNOLDVS VINCEMIVS.   pag: 96.

Hier wird D. Hantbroek sampt den seinigen nieder gemacht.

Hier werden ihnen die Nasen und Ohren auch die Mannheit abgeschnitten.

Die Vestung Seeland auff der Tyawan gelegen.

Baxenboy.

Hier werden sie theils erwürget theils hin weg geiaget.

Hier werden sie an die Creutz geschlagen.

Hier Opfern die Chinesen ihrem Abgott Iossien.

Die Insul Formosa 60. Deutscher M.

D. LEONARDVS KAMPEN. D. PETRVS MVS.

Hier werden die Weibsbilder Erstlich ge-
schändet vnd hernach Ermordet.

Hier werden den Leuthen Händ vnd Füsse ab gehaue
vnd so Iammerlich hingerichtet.

Hier werden sie theils Ritter gemacht v. theils in die wildnus verjagt.

Hier werden sie an die Bäume ge nagelt
vnd enthäust.

Hier werden die Schwangern weiber auf geschnite.

2. *Engraving of the Dutch fort Zeelandia surrounded by scenes of violence done to Dutch subjects when Zheng Chenggong landed. The top shows Dutch martyrs killed by the Chinese. It was originally engraved by C. Van Pas in 1663, entitled,* A short and concise account of the events on Formosa: The island Taiwan and Fort Zeelandia on July 5th, 1661.

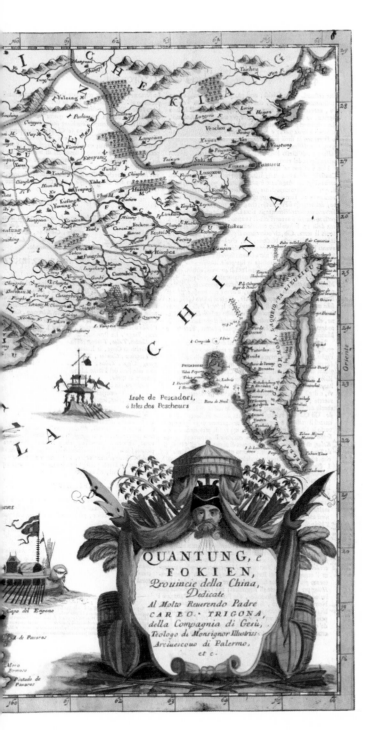

3. *The China coast and Taiwan. The river on Taiwan's east coast first appeared on this map. Vincenzo Coronelli, 1696.*

Fort de Zeelande ou de Taiovang

P.

4. *From Seygert van Regteren's 1635 Version of Cadidius Account of the Island. This is
the earliest picture of the Dutch fort on Taiwan.*

Naves e China et Iava velis ex arundine
contextis et anchoris ligneis.

Schepen van China en Iava met rieten
seylen en houten anckers

32 en 33

5. *"A Chinese or Javanese boat with reed sails and wooden anchors." A print from Jan Huygen van Linschoten's* A History of the Navigation to the East Indies, *published posthumously in 1619.*

ABITANTI DELL'ISOLA DI FORMOSA

6. *Taiwan aborigines by Italian engraver And. Bernieri. Despite the aborigines nakedness both European and Chinese artists drew them with clothes.*

諸羅縣蕭壠等社熟番
諸羅縣為曰蕭壠社曰加溜灣社曰麻豆社曰哆咯嘓社服飾大略與諸羅
等社同男以竹片束腹曰箍肚裳其新細錄載折為簡長三尺以鼻吹之歲
時婦女多以鐵銅相倛銅又按府志哆咯嘓社男女成婚後俱折去上齒各
二彼此護藏蓋示終身不改之意云諸羅縣各社歲輸丁賦一百八十餘兩

7. Chinese painting of aborigines. The man on the right is playing a nose pipe. Ashamed of their nakedness, the Chinese drew the aborigines clothed.

8. *Aborigine drinking festivities. Also notice the houses in the background. Yu took a particular interest in the Taiwan aborigines' homes describing them in great detail for his Chinese audience. From Taiwan Fanshe Fengsu, eighteenth century.*

9. *Aborigine receiving tattoos. All male aborigines took tattoos on their chest, back and arms. Yu describes the more exotic, such as chests with leapords and biceps with skulls. From* Taiwan Fanshe Fengsu, *eighteenth century.*

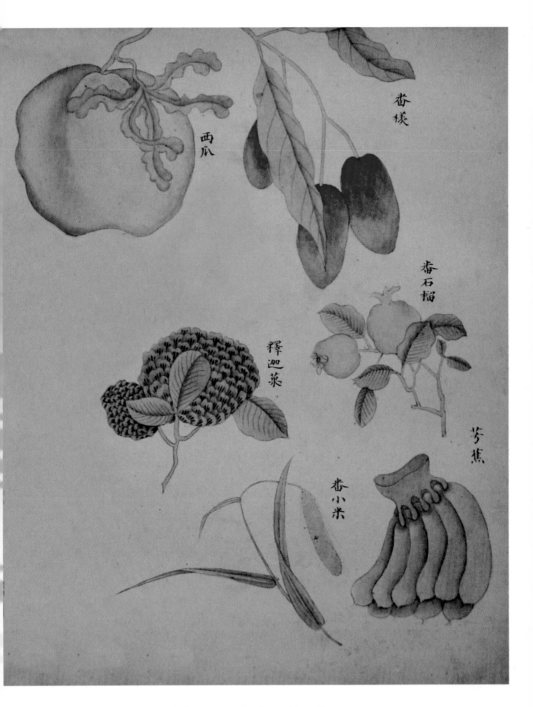

番檨

西瓜

番石榴

釋迦菓

芳蕉

番小米

10. Taiwan had a surprising abundance of fruit. This painting
  includes a rare depiction of mangos (center top). Despite Yu's
  dislike of the bananas, later settlers took a liking to them. All,
  including Yu, did like the watermelon (upper left corner). From
  Taiwan Fanshe Fengsu, eighteenth century.

11. *Portrait of a Qing official.*

The only line that separates the "raw" from the "cooked" is where the hills begin and the plains end. Sometimes the mountain aborigines will rush out of the hills, kill and burn Chinese and the villages of the cooked aborigines, then return from whence they came. When this happens there is no line.

The villagers advise Yu not to enter the raw aborigine territory across the plain and into the mountain. Such warnings only excite Yu who decides he must look at what lies beyond that mountain in front of him. They tell him that "the raw aborigines often hide in the hills to hunt deer. Even if they see a person their arrows will fly. Do not go!" Yu does not reply. He nods as if in agreement then finds a suitable walking stick and sets off.

The foliage is unbelievably thick. Yu cannot find a path through the forest floor, as it is littered with decaying trees and vines and moss. Branches and rocks and an overgrowth of shrubs leave no walking route, not even a place for Yu to place his feet. Growth on the forest canopy is so dense that it blocks out the sun, leaving Yu in the dark beneath a vegetation ceiling. "Looking up I can only see a small patch of blue sky. In front of me I know there is a mountain but the trees block it from view." He hears a river but cannot find it. A wind blows through the forest giving Yu a slight chill.

The forest wildlife does not welcome its visitor. Orangutans swing from the trees and scream and throw rocks. Old Orangutans the size of small children sit looking angrily at their intruder, as if he had invaded their home. Snakes on the forest floor hiss, wrapping around the dead branches on the ground and threatening the leg of anything that moves within their striking distance.

Yu has had enough. He is adventurous but the snakes have shattered his nerves. He turns around trying to find the same route back.

JUNE 6

SHALU

"Rain, again. Heavy mist. Clothes all wet like they have just been washed. The trail has turned to mud so thick I can't move my feet through it. Utterly depressing," Yu writes.

Suspended between the soggy sky and mushy ground is a thick humid air. It sets about the party as if it will never leave, instilling Yu with fears that he will never get dry again. Everything has become completely saturated to the point where the clothes on his body stick to the skin. Yu writes a poem:

> Savages' houses like the nests of ants,
>   low thatched roofs without a boon.
> The mist blowing in the windows
>   and bringing the sea into the room.
> I escape the rain leaving footprints.
>   It drenches the beds where we stoop.
> The river rises and we must stop
>   stuck like chickens in a coop.

Later that day an aborigine woman wanders into the village. Her disheveled hair falls over a face that appears un-human to the Chinese travelers. She waves her arms frantically like she needs something. Yu gives her food but the other aborigines drive her away. "She's a witch," they say. "She will work magic on people. Don't let her get close to you!"

JUNE 7

SHALU

The weather has finally cleared and Yu rises early in great delight. If the weather holds then the water will reside within two or three days and they can cross the gushing river in front of them. They have already come at least half way to their destination in the north of the island. The road ahead is not long.

After their noon meal Yu can hear the sound of the southern wind. It blows through the village and dries the damp clothes still sticking to Yu's back.

Soon the south wind does more than just frolic through the leaves and blow the moisture out of Yu's shirts. It turns to heavy gusts, bending the trees in half and the grass to the ground. Yu begins to fear that such a wind will destroy his ships if they have not yet arrived in Danshui. He hopes the ships have made it to Danshui, otherwise they will meet a terrible fate. Yu begins to worry about Wang.

As the light fades and evening falls over the land a villager arrives from the coast. "I saw two large ships sailing north," he says. Now Yu knows that the ships did not wait in the safety of the Lu-er-men harbor. Yu knows that they tried to sail north before the winds and rains came. He is worried. The possibility that his ships have not arrived in Danshui becomes even more plausible; the possibility that his ships have been blown up against the cragged Taiwan coast.

He sits outside alone with his anxiety, the heavy wind unable to carry his worries away from him. The harder it whips around his robe covered shoulders the more he worries. It is midnight before Yu lays down, but still he cannot sleep.

JUNE 8

SHALU

In the afternoon the wind dies down but Yu's trepidation does not. Gu tells Yu to relax. "Don't worry about the two ships! They cannot sail if there is no south wind, and it has been a long time since any south wind. Yesterday the wind blew like mad making it unwise to sail. Why be worried?"

The aborigines say that the water level of the rivers still remain deep from the runoffs and unsafe to cross.

JUNE 11

WANLI VILLAGE

They have been stuck in Shalu for over twenty days now. Not only is Yu worried about the ships but he is also restless. He has waited long enough. Raging river or not, Yu demands that they push northward.

They walk 10 kilometers to the river. Under the weight of their baggage and Yu's cart, the aborigine porters are pushed beneath the surface of the river. "Although we avoid drowning, we have to walk completely through the water," Yu writes. Within 200 meters they cross three more rivers.

The trail northward is deserted. All the houses along the roadside are abandoned. "We can't even find a drink of water," Yu says. When they finally see someone on the trail it comes as a great delight.

The party goes to Wanli Village for the night.

They have arrived early and Yu has some time to record his reflections on the aborigines: "After crossing the rivers, the face of the savages driving the cart are uglier. The tattoos on their chest and back become that of leopards. Both the men and the women cut their hair in bangs to their forehead in the shape of a top. They use tree bark for hats. The women savages have five holes in their ears, for which the decorate with conch and cowrie shells. They walk very fast, faster than the men."

Yu has also seen and heard much discrimination against the aborigines, which he finds unacceptable. "Just because they are different does not mean we must discriminate against them." He criticizes officials and interpreters, saying that "they have no clothes, so you say they don't get cold; they stand in the rain and sleep outside so you say they don't get sick; they walk great distances with heavy loads, and you say they can endure excruciating work. Please! How can you say these things? They are still people, their flesh and blood the same as ours. You don't run horses at night, nor do you overstrain oxen, because they will get sick and die. If horses and oxen are like this then people are even more vulnerable." Yu says that people may differ in appearance but their nature is all the same. He says we all enjoy eating a full meal and want warmth and rest. "This is human nature. The wise know this."

Laboring Taiwan aborigines. Eighteenth-century Chinese painting.

THE QING AS COLONIZERS

So determined to maintain a status quo in transfering power from the Zheng era, the Qing dynasty did not even include the aborigines in the standard tax holidays or tax reduction measures. In fact, the aborigine head tax brought in some of the highest revenues for the Qing government and they continued to press it not individually, as a head tax customarily was leveled, but as fixed quotas on villages. The Qing managed to squeeze around eight thousand taels out of the aborigine tribes annually.[4] Payment demands from the natives never ceased. As one seventeenth-century contemporary noted, "the aborigines are very stupid and afraid of the law, allowing officials to exploit them."

An early eighteenth-century Taiwan county magistrate estimated that in addition to the required official taxes, tribes paid out eight thousand taels in gifts to officials, four thousand taels in hemp, and two thousand taels in salt.[5] Other kickbacks also burdened the aborigines even after the government cracked down on the corrupt practice also terrorizing the Chinese settlers. Official censor Chen Bin said that he had "investigated and every year the savages must give large kickbacks. The amount depends on the size of the village, running from 280 taels per village to 120 taels, 80 taels, 60 taels, 40 taels and on down are all common demands."[6] Yu said the entire government took "advantage of the simplicity of the savages and want very much for them to be poor."[7]

In addition, officials placed a heavy labor service on the aborigines, forcing them regardless of weather or terrain to drive carts and carry sedan chairs. Because the aborigines did not have the habit of using money, the interpreters would force them to perform tasks, no matter how large or menial and no matter if they were men, women or children. "They make them labor without rest," Yu observed. Chen Bin said that "they are flogged like slaves even though they too are children of the heavenly dynasty." Yet in the same breath he reminded how adept the natives were at carrying documents over long distances and leading oxcarts to transport timber.[8] This is probably why his proposals to level fees for aborigine services would go unheeded for twelve years and allowed censor Huang Shuqing to write that whenever any official or soldier, no matter how petty, went on tour, they forced aborigines to carry their luggage and sedan chair, "labors so harsh they had to flee for their lives!"[9]

Tribes did complain bitterly about Qing interpreters exhorting fees that exceeded two or three times the official tax obligation. They took anything of value the tribe owned and demanded sex from aborigine women. The problems began with the magistrates who would demand payments from the interpreters, who would subsequently turn around and demand payment from the aborigines. "Everyday of every month they exploit them," Chen Bin exclaimed. "They make every family go without clothes and every child without food. They exploit them right down to the bone."[10] Yu said the interpreters doubled as tax collectors, and "had ways to tax all barbarian goods and products." The serene character of Father De Mailla on travels throughout Taiwan in the early eighteenth century would call the interpreters "unworthy harpies who pray upon [the aborigines] pitilessly: indeed, they are such petty tyrants that they drive even the patience of the mandarins."[11]

Most of the interpreters were actually criminals that had fled from the China mainland to escape officials and a probable death sentence. After some years on Taiwan, on the frontier among the aborigines, they learned the language and came to act as interpreters. "They learn how to exploit the savages," Yu said. When the father dies, the son takes over so "generation after generation they go on exploiting the savages." The tax collectors changed every one to two years but the interpreters never changed and it was in their interest to keep the aborigines stupid and poor. "If they are stupid, then they don't know any rights or morals and can be cheated; if they are poor, then the interpreters can easily threaten them and they cannot fight back." The interpreters tried to turn officials against the aborigines by giving wrong translations and not informing aborigines of the laws. This, in turn, made the aborigines scared of the interpreters and forced them to treat the "harpies" like kings. "The world's worst off people are not as bad as the Taiwan savages," Yu said.

All in good imperialist humor, for "if we request something the barbarians will give it; if the barbarians break the law they are beaten but still they do not hate us greatly." If the barbarians did not hate their rulers greatly, they did resent them. Throughout Qing rule, revolts were not uncommon—from the innocent beheading of an official who demanded a daughter for marriage to the full scale slaughter of settler villages. The largest revolt came in 1731 when a subprefect ordered aborigine men to supply timber for the construction of a new government post and the women to run the oxcarts.

More Chinese meant more abuses. Tribes complained of officials sleeping with their women, and soldiers raiding the food stores. When the women refused to pull the oxcarts the subprefect beat them with rattan strips. This was the last straw, evidently. That year the tribes revolted; attacking the subprefect and setting the officials on fire. They killed all the Chinese settlers and burnt their villages to the ground.[12] Chen Bin warned about such uprisings even before they happened: "the aborigines are poor and tired, if this goes on they will certainly revolt. We should give them peace and let them work and rest like normal human beings."[13] More than a century after Chen Bin, the Qing military commander in Danshui in 1887 reminded his officials that "the aborigines have been cheated often. If we give them no justice there will certainly be no peace."[14]   ∽

The Formosan coast is a devil. Danger is everywhere as if it cost nothing...we already call it The Tomb of the Anchors. On the bottom there could be a lot of money worth [of anchors]. If only the fishes could use them as toothpicks.

UNKNOWN FRENCH SAILOR

船
難

PART 6

Shipwreck

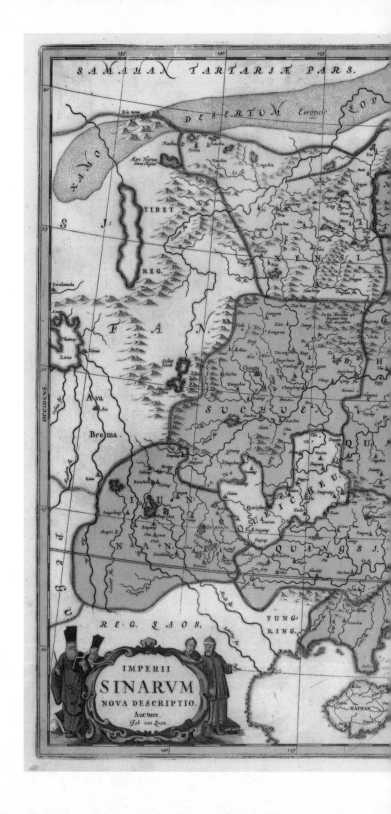

Dutch map of China based on the Chinese map Guang Yu Tu.
By Jacob van Loon, 1658.

From The Illustrated London News, *1890.*

Shipwreck

ON THE TRAIL NORTHWARDS

On the trail near Houlong Village Yu and his party see a motley figure stumbling in the opposite direction. As they grow closer they see his clothes are torn and he is limping heavily. He is a Chinese. Yu recognizes his travel companion Wang Yunsen!

"The boat was wrecked and our bodies thrown into the water," Wang says in a whimper. "I am lucky to see you again."

Astonished, Yu bluntly asks why he did not die. Wang tells Yu his story:

"I boarded the boat on the third [May 22] and we anchored in Lu-er-men waiting for the south wind. On the eighteenth [June 6] we had a light breeze and set sail. Within a day, the mast and the sail were not in harmony and we were forced into the black waters. The ship's bow dove into the ocean and great waves crashed together over it, striking great terror in the hearts

| 123

of the sailors. They prayed to the goddess Mazu. With no harbor to anchor we were in panic throughout the night.

"The nineteenth was the same as the day before. After noon, the south wind picked up and drove us forward. It was if the heavens were helping us. Soon the wind began to blow tremendously, but because the helm had broken, it would not accept orders, and forcing it only broke it into three pieces.

"The wind brought thousands of butterflies to dance around our ship. The sailors took it as a bad omen. At the shenke hour* [4pm] the wind slowed down and hundreds of black birds flocked to the boat and could not be driven off. The sailors called it bad augury. They burned paper money and prayed to the gods, but the birds would still not leave. Even when we tried to capture them they would not leave; just squawk squawking as if they were trying to talk to us.

"After a short time the wind picked up again in great gusts and threatened to drive us under. We prayed to Mazu, pleading for a divination to keep the ship safe from harm. The goddess did not agree. We asked her to save us from death. The goddess agreed. We rid the ship of a third of its goods. Towards the second watch we saw a small harbor in the distance. Everyone was happy that we made it alive but the water was too shallow and the ship could not enter, so we anchored at the mouth of the harbor. The sailors were exhausted and everyone slept.

"At the fifth watch we lost anchor. The ship had nothing left to tie it down so we floated out to the open sea. The waves struck the ship and the rudder broke. The stern split and then we all knew that there was nothing that could be done.

" 'Only rowing can take us to shore and save us from death!' The captain shouted. Each man took up an oar and rowed vigorously. They chanted and shouted in sync just like the dragon boat festival competitions. Only when the ocean becomes dangerous and it is impossible to get close to the shore do sailors use this way.

---

* A traditional Chinese way of telling time.

"As the boat approached the shore, the waves broke it to pieces. [We] were all thrown into the water. Fortunately we could swim and did not drown. The waves swept me to shore. I looked back to where the ship once was to see only broken boards and splintered wood tossed about in the foam."

When Wang finishes his tale Yu asks about the second junk.

"How can I know?" Wang says. "That boat is more manageable so that by the eighteenth it was already a few hundred li* ahead of us."

Yu is worried and utterly discouraged. He now knows the tales of Taiwan's coast are not just campfire stories. He fears that his other ship is also lost to the crashing waves and white foam; splintered against the rocks of some alcove on the Taiwan coast. If the second ship is gone then the mission has failed. Yu is utterly discouraged. He considers giving up the mission and returning.

But Yu is not a quitter. He looks inside of himself and says silently: "We have already come over a thousand li; with only three days from our destination, how can I not continue and at least see if the other ship is safe?"

JUNE 13, MIDDAY
THE NORTHWEST COAST

Yu shares his cart with Wang. They cross over three mountains and into Zhonggang Village for lunch. Yu observes an ox trapped in a wooden cage too small for its body. Its feet are tied and it cannot stand up. The aborigines say that that it is a wild ox recently captured. "We use this method to domesticate it. The ox pulling your cart was once a wild ox," they say.

These wild ox roam the hills in packs of hundreds. They graze in the

---

* A li is a measure of distance equivalent to half a kilometer. It sometimes called a Chinese mile.

mountains, and not fearing people, their beady red eyes frighten settlers. Aborigines build pens from bamboo and herd the wild oxen into the enclosures where they starve them into submission, administering periodic beatings. As the oxen grow tame they are fed beans and sugar cane.[1]

The Chinese officials buy oxen from the aborigines, a wild one for half the price of a tamed one. The tough skin of the wild oxen make good clothing, but the Chinese use the animals as beasts of burden, forcing them to pull carts all around the island. While high officials will ride in the sedan chair, carried by aborigines under the whip, lower officials all travel by oxcart. Sending anything over great distances, and even regular people traveling to distant places on the island, require an ox-driven cart. It is such that every house has an ox fed with sugarcane.[2]

Later observers of the Taiwan oxen estimated that the packs of the animals roaming wild number well over one thousand, but by then the encroaching settlements had begun to diminish the plains and settlers soon drove the animals to extinction.[3]

After lunch the party walks through a small harbor, through the sand and water for over 15 kilometers. Wang points out where his ship had sunk and where he swam ashore. The wood debris still frolics in the surf.

They cross a deep river into Zhuqian Village. The water flows very fast and one of Yu's servants falls into the river. He is barely saved.

"When we all arrived on the opposite shore, the color had drained from all our faces," Yu writes.

JUNE 13, LATE AFTERNOON
ZHUQIAN VILLAGE (HSINCHU)

Travelers have arrived from Danshui and Jilong. They tell Yu that after the strong winds of the seventh and eighth, a junk arrived in Danshui. Yu is at once relieved and overjoyed. The mission to mine sulfur will continue.

Yu tells Wang he must return to where his ship ran aground and broke apart. Yu tells Wang he must retrieve as many of the supplies as he can. He says that the woks and the cooking utensils are sure to be recoverable. "One boat has arrived; there is no reason to give up. Don't be afraid to return to the sea once more!"

This is not a place for people.

YU YONGHE

nta que mira achina dista del puerto
leguas

aquiƒefortiƒica

淡

水

6. Entrada del puerto que mira
alnorte, tiene de ƒondo. 14.
braƒas yba diſminuyendo
haſta. 2. Ymedia

Puerto donde surgen los
nauios

Enƒenada
dista del pu

3 braſas ½

braſas

Rancheria Delos naturales

Enƒenada de S
Vista del puerto. 5

PART 7

The North.

The Spanish.

MONTES GRANDES

Ð MVCHA MADERA

Danshui.

A late seventeenth-century Chinese map of Taiwan. The original is 6.5 meters long and illustrates the entire west coast. This portion shows the north of the island.

The Spanish fort in Jilong, by Pedro de Vera, 1626.

The North. The Spanish. Danshui.

Yu leaves Wang at Zhuqian and heads over the pass. He walks some 50 kilometers without seeing even one person. The land is barren of trees; "possessed," as Yu says, "of only woods and grass." In order to cook, they dig a pit in the earth and eat under the sun. Over lunch the aborigines tell Yu that at one time this area had many peoples of many tribes. They all resisted the Dutch, who beat them and their supporters to death.

The Dutch, however, found that these tribes "do not tolerate any of the inhabitants that have already been pacified with the Company to enter their territory without risking their lives."[1] The Dutch launched strong punitive expeditions, punishing the non-subservient tribes. But they did not exterminate the inhabitants; that task was left to the Zhengs.

The central plains aborigines resisted Zheng rule. They refused to pay the heavy taxes and to carry documents and supplies over great distances. In 1670, Zheng general Liu Guoxuan led an army north to punish the tribes. They "killed until almost no one was left," Yu says the inhabitants recall.[2] In fact, only six aborigines remained. They fled to the coast to hide while the surrounding tribes who heard of the massacre moved far inland.[3] Order was maintained and obedience instilled. The rest of the villages dared not to rebel.

Yet twelve years later the aborigines could take the harsh Zheng rule no longer and once again revolted. It came as Shi Lang prepared his attack and the Zhengs were frantically trying to fortify the island. Officials forced the northern aborigines to carry supplies into Danshui, but the road was poor and the officials beat them. The aborigines rose up, killing the officials and stealing the supplies. Zhuqian and other northern villages joined the revolt."That road, no one walks over," the locals said. Outraged, the Zheng rulers sent a punitive force against the rebellious tribes, forcing the abor-igines into the mountains. The army didn't dare enter the hills so they built a wall of bamboo stakes around the forests caging in the tribes. Starved into sub-mission, the tribes surrendered to a murderous army that set about exting-uishing them.[4]

Fifty years later, the Taiwan Fu Magistrate passed through the area and composed a sorrowful but obstinate poem of the exanimate land:

Dangerous savage villages, now almost extinct.
  New names for those still alive to reinstate.
Half of the savages husbandless, they can no longer give birth.
  Oh, these savages, victim to our universal truth.[5]

The aborigines that Yu meets tell him that "the Dutch were very strong. If we refused to submit, then no one was left. But the Dutch were scared of the Zhengs and fled. Now the Zhengs have been extinguished by the Qing and all their soldiers are gone. This emperor is the strongest." Lessons have been learned; unpopulated land and aborigine obedience show for it.[6]

Despite the lack of people on the land, Yu sees many deer. He learns that Taiwan has three types of deer. The aborigines in his party catch one of each kind. They use the skins to pay taxes or trade them for other goods. The Zhengs collected an average of 60,000 skins a year from the aborigines in taxes. Before them, the Dutch cashed in on the Japanese market, which had a great demand for leather used in soldiers' uniforms. The best year for the Dutch saw exports in excess of 150,000 skins, but annual trade averaged about 40,000 to 50,000 skins for the company.

The aborigines tell Yu that they judge the age of the deer by their antlers, one point for each year of age. Yu says he has heard of deer with five hundred to one thousand points on their antlers, "but that is just nonsense. The aborigines have lived here for many generations and they rarely see more than seven points."[7]

Taiwan has no tigers in the hills so the deer propagate. In fact they mate like rabbits. "They are a perverted animal," Yu says. "I hear they will mate in great orgies, though I have never seen it." He says that the mother doe will watch her young until they grow up, then leave them out of fear of internal mating. This, however, is not a strong enough precaution. Yu says, "the only animal that won't commit incest is the horse. If it does, it will kill itself."[8]

Before the village of Nankan, Yu and his party plunge into the forest. The path disappears beneath thick woods and brush and the aborigine guides must cut a trail. Even so, the branches claw at the travelers' hats and clothes. Yu stumbles into a foxhole and cries, "this is not a place for people."

JUNE 15

DANSHUI

From Nankan they march over the hill to the sea. Foam from the waves washes up to the wheels of the cart and dampens Yu's skirt.

They arrive in Bali Village, where they are blocked by another river. It is the Danshui River. At three kilometers wide it is one of the largest rivers in northern Taiwan. All the mountain creeks and runoffs flow into it before pushing out to sea. Because of the coral growing at the mouth, which appears and disappears with the height of the tide, ocean junks fear this spot.

In the sand on the bank of the river, Yu and his party find a small aborigine dugout canoe. It fits two people and they slowly row themselves across to the other side. The Danshui Village chief, Big Zhang, is waiting for them.

Yu also finds his ship at anchor in the Danshui harbor.

Spanish map of the South China Sea, including the Fujian coast, Taiwan and the island of Manila. By Pedro de Vera, 1626.

SPANIARDS IN TAIWAN

Yu recalls that the "Red Hair Barbarians built a castle here." The castle is still visible on the hillside looking out over the harbor and mouth of the river. Today the Qing conquerors no longer fear bandits and so do not keep a military force in the north. Danshui has housed no troops for many years and the military equipment looks old and useless, but no one knows for sure. Every half year Taiwan Fu will send a patrol up to stay one night and return the next day.

The red hair barbarians Yu refers to were the Spanish, not the Dutch. Fearing their European competitors would disrupt trade between China and the Philippines, the Spanish arrived in northern Taiwan to keep the Dutch in check, and, as the Philippine governor put it in a letter to the King, "to enjoy the benefits of close trade with China, that would redound to the productivity of the neighboring island."[9] The Spanish fort went up in 1629 to act as a base for the traders, and for protection from the constantly attacking aborigines. "May our Lord grant us the means to pacify and convert this island," the Spanish governor in Manila wrote home to his King.[10]

The King consented and in their pacification efforts the Spaniards pumped in half a million in some unnamed currency, which went to sustaining 300 Spanish soldiers, 220 ordinary troops, and 100 soldiers from the Philippine provinces of Nueva Segovia and Pampanga. The money also kept some vessels manned by the sailors to accompany the artillery needed to defend those forts.[11] Although the council had its doubts about the results of these expenditures, the Spanish missionaries continued to lobby Manila for more funds for further infrastructure projects, such as hospitals and schools, citing the need to begin the establishment of a colony.[12]

The priests folded these requests into their reports on the successes and failures of converting the aborigines. As a whole the Spanish found the aborigine population "somewhat inept and slow but naturally candid and simple...Some are extremely greedy and constantly go about begging." The missionaries found room to complain of the aborigines drunkenness as "their primary vice." Fr. Esquivel relates tales of wild feasts that went on for "three full days, day and night, during which they do nothing else but *masitanguitanguich*—that is, to sing and dance, with jars of wine all around; they drink all the time. Some collapse and fall asleep, and then go on with the revelry as soon as they wake up. They eat seafood and raw venison. They are a filthy lot who eat deer entrails without first cleaning them of excrement." The frequent infanticide by which the mothers would bury babies alive or trade them for stones, clothing or other goods, only deepened the European convictions of the need to impose the ways of the West upon the savages.[13]

Conversion efforts did not go off smoothly, however. Reports back to the council in Manila note that the natives "convert more out of a particular intent to sell fish than out of their interest in the religion itself...For once these natives return to their own, they mock and deride the ceremonies of our holy catholic faith."[14] Fr. Esquivel explained it as a fear of the European invaders, noting that "they are still extremely afraid and suspicious of us. Up to now they have a deep-seated fear of the Spaniards. When I first came, they spread rumors that I carried shackles in a pouch to bind them and take them as prisoners to Manila. They directly accused me of this once, in the presence of another priest. They asked where my wife, children and possessions were. When I told them that priests neither get married nor own anything, they called me a big liar and a deceiver. The same thing happened —what's more they thought me insane—when I tried to explain to them from the catechism that we will all rise from the dead."[15]

These were the more subdued reactions to the Spanish presence. The more agitated ones were direct hostilities, such as the fate that befell a small Spanish party out buying rice. The Spanish saw it coming, and had earlier noted that"some natives were on the move—many of whom were professed enemies of these lands." As a precaution they sent a reinforcement of twenty soldiers out with the rice-buying party. Though it helped little; three hundred aborigine warriors hid along the mountainside, concealed among the soil and foliage, lying in wait for the Europeans. When the purchasing party drew near, the aborigines sprang from their cover and "showered them with one and many arrows," killing twelve soldiers, a score of laborers, two women and some young boys. Fr. Luis got an arrow through the side and another one through his heart, bringing the God-fearing man to the ground dead. The soldiers had no time to react as the aborigines "had already wreaked havoc even before their presence was felt." The Spanish fled back to the fort leaving the body of their kinsmen on the spot for twelve days before they dared to venture forth and retrieve them—minus the hands, feet and head, of course.[16] Two months later, Danshui tribes attacked the fort one night, setting it on fire and driving out sixty Spaniards, thirty of whom the aborigines ambushed and killed.[17]

The Spanish met utter failure in their trade operations as well. The port, it seems, had acquired a"very bad reputation," as Fr. Esquivel put it. Japanese merchants didn't want to come to Jilong to trade as hoped because "they do not find in this island the price sought." The Father went on to term the whole situation a "commercial slump," though there was never any boom to compliment it. The largest returns were six hundred bundles of cloth that arrived unregistered on something they called a patache, but only thirty-nine of the bundles could be sold for a total profit of four to five thousand pesos.[18] The treasury at the Jilong fort was constantly in debt and famine frequently broke out among the Europeans stationed there due to the lack of funds to buy rice and the extended periods with no supply ship. Furthermore, the unbearable climate sent most of the Spanish residents back to the more agreeable beaches of the Philippines. The Manila council noted one session that the post "has yielded little or no fruit at all in the eleven years since its establishment, and that it has caused His Majesty great expense to maintain it."[19] The council recommended withdrawal from the island.

That was in 1637. In fact, opposition to a colony had begun much earlier, before the fort was even built. In 1627, Juan Cevicos, the captain and skipper of the Manila Galleons, warned against setting up a port on Taiwan."That island is not of importance to us, either for its own products or for commerce with China," he said. He noted that Spain already had the Philippines and did not require a half-way station, especially in a"poor and barren land," as he described Taiwan.[20] Even years after their settlement, the parties had much to regret, as the Manila governor testified in his letter to the King in late 1634: "I dare not say that the forts in Isla Hermosa must be abandoned, but I constantly affirm that it would have been good that they never started."[21]

Under pressure from such views, and wanting to focus on the Philippine campaign, the governor-general in Manila began downsizing the Danshui operations in 1638, calling back almost all the troops stationed there so that only fifty to sixty men remained. In a concurrent motion, they began pulling apart Fort Santo Domingo in Danshui and hauling it piece by piece over to Jilong to reinforce Fortress Santisima Trinidad on Heping island off the coast of Jilong. The Dutch took full advantage of Spain's withdrawal, launching an attack in which Dutch soldiers outnumbered the Spaniards by one hundred to one. In addition, some seven hundred natives assisted in the invasion, in which the Spanish complained that "the Dutch knew very well that we lacked men to meet them in combat, and that we had no ships."

But the Spanish held out. The Dutch landed and climbed the hill where "two war drums boomed away, while flags fluttered atop the hill and through the corridors of the village's stone church." Lacking the means for a full siege the Dutch retreated, setting the town and church on fire as they left, razing everything to the ground. The good lord then promptly dashed their ship on the Jilong rocks where it exploded into pieces.[22]

Determined to drive the Spanish off the island, the next year the Dutch sailed five ships with as many as eight hundred men back into the Jilong harbor, where "God Almighty had given us a splendid weather for landing," as a Dutch captain recalls.[23] They stormed the hill overlooking the Spanish fort and set up two eighteen-pound cannons which proceeded to shell the Spaniards with 108 rounds in a day. Combined with continuous musket fire "the situation looked like judgment day" to the Spanish priests trapped inside.[24]

Such a volley of force by the Dutch knocked down fort walls and made it clear that "in a short time they were completely defeated," as a combatant wrote of the Spanish troops. But the Spanish locked themselves in and prepared for a siege which continued for "six days of bloody and obstinate fighting." When all was said and done, the Dutch kept the Spaniards as prisoners and won twenty heavy pieces of artillery, gunpowder and ammunition, warlike stores, twenty-five thousand dollars, and mercantile goods, in total worth over one million dollars.[25]

A wonderful war prize, but, for all the same reasons that the Spanish found a burden, the Dutch too soon discovered it was "nothing but trouble," as a company official put it. Trade was not forthcoming and the aborigines continued to hunt Dutchmen just as they did Spaniards. The Dutch abandoned Jilong in 1668.[26]   CB

If you mix together sulfur, realger, and saltpeter then ignite them, fire will spurt forth burning your hands, face, and even your house!

NINTH-CENTURY DAOIST BOOK OF CHEMICAL FORMULAS

As the poor Indians lookt upon the Spaniards as more than Men, because the knowledge they had of the properties of Nitre, Sulphur and Charcoale duly mixed, enabled them to Thunder and Lighten so fatelly, when they pleas'd.

ROBERT BOYLE

硫

磺

PART 8

Sulfur

Early eighteenth-century Chinese map of the Taipei basin. The lake in the center was caused by an earthquake in 1694, according to Yu.

Sulfur fields in the northern Taiwan hills, 1868.

Sulfur

Big Zhang has informed Yu that the houses he requested build are finished. Yu takes Gu and his servants up the Danshui River to look at them. Their boat passes through a narrow point in the river and into a body of water so large that Yu "can't see the banks." Big Zhang tells Yu that three years ago last May an earthquake shook the island changing the landscape. "The land collapsed and the water rushed in to fill it," he says.

This is the Taipei basin, surrounded on all sides by tall mountains. Yu says it is filled with water. The river basin here used to support three aborigine villages, but the inhabitants have all moved away. Big Zhang points out bamboo groves protruding from the water. He says that is where the aborigines used to live. After the earthquake, Big Zhang says, the aborigines will not live near the hills, and have all gone downriver. "Is it possible that the sea has become fields?" Yu asks quoting an old Chinese adage, spooked by the possibility of its reality.

Some three hundred years later Yu's lake no longer exists, replaced by metropolitan Taipei, and some even doubt that it ever did. Not that Yu is mistaken, only that he is too vague in the language he uses. The entire Taipei basin is not filled with water, only flooded near Guandu where the Jilong River meets the Xindian River to form the Danshui River and moves out to sea. In 1708 people began farming in the upper basin right where the lake was supposed to sit.[1]

At the base of a hill facing the water, Yu can see the houses Big Zhang built for him. They stand in the middle of a grass meadow with their entrances all pointing in different directions. Due to the unevenness of the land, Big Zhang could not build them in a uniform fashion. Big Zhang has built twenty houses, which Yu will divide up among his extracting party. Two will be used for the big woks, six for the sulfur, seven to house the workers, and two for the cooks. Yu, Gu and the servants will have three among them.

Yu hears the sound of falling water and thinks a great waterfall must be nearby. He searches all day but can find none.

JUNE 22
BEITOU

Wang returns from salvaging the shipwreck. He has recovered seventy-two tools and the caldron.

JUNE 23
YU'S CAMP, BEITOU

The chiefs of twenty-three aborigine villages come to see Yu. These villages are all prefectures of the main Danshui village. Yu intoxicates them with diluted wine and spoils them with pure sugar. He gives them rolls of cloth and they leave happy.

Yu figures he can trade cloth for sulfur. Seven pieces of cloth can get him one pound of sulfur-rich dirt. Yu estimates he has enough cloth to bring in some 278 catties worth of sulfur.

JUNE 24

YU'S CAMP

Both men and women of the aborigine tribes deliver Yu his dirt in hopes of receiving the Chinese cloth. In fact, Yu is happy to clothe them. Throughout the trip he has noticed many naked aborigines. He has been half embarrassed and half disgusted by their nakedness. He notes that neither the men nor the women wear any clothes, "only cover their privates with a cloth." Dutch explorer Elie Ripon said the women go "nude apart from a little loincloth of one by a half foot which they turn in front when they talk to you and turn behind when they walk away, like a curtain...The men also go naked like they were born from the womb of their mothers, and sport their penises which look like those of a big donkey." [2]

The Dutch East India Company's early minister Reverand Georgius Candidius also observed the aborigines' nakedness, which he felt made them a "savage, rude and barbaric people," who "walk about stark-naked, without any shame and without covering up those membra qua natura ipsa vult tecta." [3] Yu notes that in winter they wear sweaters made from grass. It's a simple garment with a hole for the head. The women sometimes sew up the sides. Sometimes they wear a cut-off shirt, which leaves the stomach exposed, and a short skirt that ends above the knees. They always go without shoes. "To see them without clothes and say they don't get cold misses the point...if they had cloth perhaps they would use it," Yu says. "If they could rest they would not run around working, especially for these interpreters." [4]

Everyday the aborigines bring dirt to Yu's camp giving the Chinese explorer much time to interact with and observe local customs and culture. Their eating habits, for instance, surprise Yu. Although the ground produces five types of grain the aborigines only eat rice, corn and panicled millet. They do not eat grain. In fact, only when its time to eat do they husk the rice, not planning or storing anything. "When they wake in the morning they wait until breakfast before threshing. When it is ready then the family comes and they all eat with their hands. They hunt elk and deer in the hills, and drink the blood and eat the meat raw just to satisfy their stomachs," Yu writes.

He is awed by this whimsical nature, finding that the aborigines worry little about the wind and rain, and when traveling afar think little about having a place to stay. "If they find something to eat they eat, if they have a place to sit they sit, when they are happy they laugh, when hurt they frown," Yu notes. He sees that they don't separate spring from summer, nor one year from the next so that when they die they don't know what age they have become.

Such practices are common, possibly because of the natives' complete self-sufficiency. "Everything they need they can make themselves, and there is nothing they do not use that they cannot make themselves," Yu writes. He finds strong hemp nets spun to catch fish and home-made bows and arrows from bamboo to hunt with. Strapped to their waist day and night, the aborigines wear a knife. Everything they make they do so with this knife. In fact, about the only thing the aborigines cannot do themselves is smelt metals to make this knife. For this they must go down to the gorge and find iron, which they hammer between two rocks. After a long time doing this it becomes a utensil.

The aborigines have no Big Zhang to build houses for them. This they must also do themselves. They construct houses in a shape that Yu finds resembling a tortoise shell. The base is three to five feet from the ground and the ridgepole covered with grass. The grass juts far out in deep eves touching the ground so that the rain cannot seep in. Underneath, the aborigines thresh grain and cook, sit and lie down. Here they store their ox-carts, fishing nets, farm tools, and posts, and even let the chickens roost. The front and rear of the house are open, and beneath the ridgepole are steps to climb up to the main room. In order to lie down one has a deerskin mat to place wherever desired. In the hot summer months like these, they take away the deerskins and just lie on the ground.

All around the houses, Yu finds buckets of wine. The aborigine method of making wine involves all the men, women, old folks and children of the tribe to chew up rice and spit it in the buckets. Within a few days it ferments and becomes wine. To drink, they mix it with spring water. As the guest, Yu observes the women first drinkng from the bucket before passing it to him for a gulp. Once Yu drank the whole bucket and his hosts were delighted. They danced and yelled. They all joined hands and sung and danced, calling on him to drink more.

If Yu's liquor tolerance is high, the aborigines' is higher. "Both the male and female savages are addicted to alcohol," Yu writes. The aborigines use much of the year's crop to brew wine. After the harvest "all the men and women drink as much as they can, they sing and shout like they are boiling. For three days and three nights they do not rest. Even if the grain is used up and they go hungry, they do not regret."

Yu has hope for the aboriginal population and he feels he is doing his part to civilize them with wine, sugar and cloth. "To teach them rules and etiquette, to educate them, to give them foresight to plan into the future; to wear clothes, eat properly, to respect marriage and the rights of society; to love one's spouse, to respect one's elders and the emperor, and to love the gods. In short, it is our duty to tame the savage in them," he says. Yu thinks it will take one hundred years at most and thirty years at least to see cultural change within the aborigines. "If we can accomplish this then they will be Chinese."

To Yu, they almost look Chinese, only "their faces not much different, eyes deeper and bigger, and language filled with 'lu-gwo-lu' sounds." The legend says that Taiwan, at one time, had no people. When the Yuan Dynasty rose to power in 1206, taking control of all of China, the peoples of the previous Jin Dynasty fled to Taiwan. After many generations they forgot their background but their language has not changed. Even so, Yu finds that they live in a primitive society, "just beating rocks everyday and lying under the sun." He thinks their illiteracy and lack of knowledge leaves them with no ideals, no purpose and unable to plan. "They don't know what season it is; when they get old they just die without any recollection of age; they wait for the cold before they find clothes, and they wait until they are hungry before they find food. They plan for nothing."

He once heard of a Chinese merchant's idea to contact and civilize the aborigines on the east coast. The merchant took a party of seven and crossed the central mountain range, sleeping during day and traveling by night to avoid the savage headhunting aborigines. They crossed through raw aborigine territory scaling many mountains before they arrived at the east coast. When they walked into the village, the villagers knew they were Chinese and invited them to their homes. They told the Chinese that"we are trapped by the raw aborigines with no means to communicate with the west coast. We want to join together with the western aborigines to fight against the central aborigines. If you can send troops to help then after the war we will become the emperor's subjects and pay taxes."

The merchant's story has no conclusion, only Yu's misconception that "the land in the east is larger than that in the west;" and his fantasies that "if the government supports the plains aborigines to fight the mountain aborigines, then we can force them to surrender." Yu wants to burn down the poisonous plants and clear the woods of all dangers making it safe and civilized."This will turn the savage people into polite and cultured people," he remarks. Yu hopes these savages will become like those of China's southern provinces whose "people were once savages but have now been civilized...breeding some great scholars of today."[5]

Yu's cultural imperialism falls in line with the history of China's rulers. It began when Chinese civilization sprouted along the banks of the Wei River and slowly moved south. The process worked on the principle of securing borders and pacifying the "barbarians"—narrowly defined as those people lacking in civilized ways—through assimilation. That is to say,

Chinese colonialism took security and protection as its fundamentals. Like the well versed Ming scholar Wang Fuzhi wrote in his treatise on the function of the emperor, "even the ants have rulers who preside over the territory of their nests and, when red ants or flying white ants penetrate their gates, the ruler organizes all his own kind to bite and kill the intruders, drive them far away from the anthill and prevent foreign interference. Thus he who rules the swarm must have the means to protect it."[6]

One could say that emperor Kangxi was merely protecting his ant hive when he took to eliminating the Zhengs and conquering Taiwan. He had no more desire to annex and occupy the island than he did to march on Rome. In fact, after the last of the Zheng resistance surrendered, admonishing defeat and accepting the rule of the Qing, Kangxi wanted to clear out the island and throw it back to the waves and rocks. Officials then referred to Taiwan as "a petty piece of dirt in the sea" which can "offer China nothing...We cannot live next to the tattooed savages. The entire operation will waste our money." They called to evacuate the island and leave the land vacant.[7] Or as the emperor himself said to his court, who continued to pester him on the problem, "Taiwan belongs to the sea and has nothing to do with us! It never had any civilization and even if it becomes appealing it is not worth ruling. We only pacified that rock because our coastlines never saw any peace!"[8]

Doubt on the decision to occupy the island still looms, and talk abounds on whether or not to dispose of Taiwan. Such talk infuriates Yu. "Must I explain the harm that would befall us if we gave up Taiwan?" The harm that would befall the China kingdom, Yu explains, would be enormous. "The Red Hair Barbarians have long term plans and we don't know what they are thinking...luckily they are far from China so they cannot easily invade. If they have Taiwan to put their feet on they can attack in the morning and return home at night."[9]

Under such a threat Yu pothers about the lack of protection for the ten west coast harbors. "Today only Lu-er-men and Anping are protected and the other harbors not valued. This is poor planning," Yu warns. "If rebels or the Red Hair Barbarians attack, they only need to block Lu-er-men. Then they can easily invade through the other harbors and set up bases. With the head and tail covered our army would be split in all directions. The whole island would be theirs!"

cs

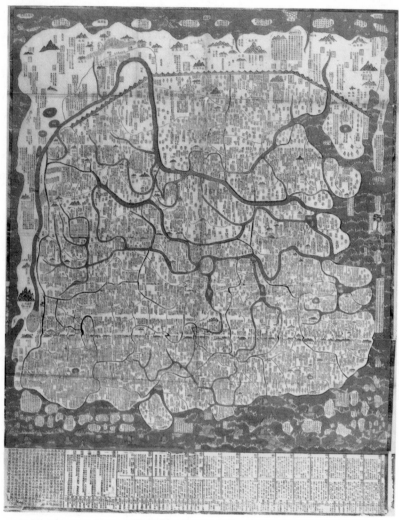

A Chinese map of the world from 1593 entitled "The Myriad of Countries of the World and Modern Human Affairs." The "myriad of countries" are the islands in the seas around China in the center. America is part of the landmass north of the Great Wall. The original woodcut measures1,325 mm x 1,725 mm.

Today Yu has more pressing matters at hand. He must extract sulfur. He asks the aborigines where they got the dirt and they all point to the mountain behind the houses. They bring him good dirt, "heavy in weight and glossy in texture." Yu says that if you can hear the sound of the texture when rubbing it between your fingers then it is good dirt. If you cannot then it is bad. But this dirt is not the finished sulfur that Yu needs. In order to extract the sulfur from the dirt he must first boil it in oil. Yu outlines his extraction technique:

First break up the dirt clumps and grind it into powder, then lay it out in the sun to dry thoroughly. Take the medium sized wok and first add ten catties or more of oil, then slowly add the dry dirt. Make a cross with large bamboo poles and place one man on each side stirring with it. When dirt makes contact with the oil, the sulfur contained within it will flow out while the oil and the dirt melt together. Continue to add dirt and add oil until the wok is full. You should be able to fit eight to nine catties of dirt in the wok, but must observe its quality to decide on how much oil to add.

Workers often use a steel ladle to extract the juice. If the remaining mud bubbles too much you must add dirt, if it does not bubble at all then you must add oil. If you do not add enough oil then all the sulfur will be lost, but if you add just the right amount and use good dirt then one wok-full will yield four hundred to five hundred catties of sulfur. If the amounts are off then you may only get one hundred to two hundred catties or even only ten. Although the key is in adding the right amounts of oil, taking care of the fire is also an important factor. It cannot be too hot otherwise all will burn, yet it can neither be too small or the sulfur will not rise.

OUT OF CHINA: GUNPOWDER

Yu's method is a bit more advanced than that described by his fore-runner Lu Zhiyi in his work in the 1630's on "How to Extract Sulfur from the Taiwan Dirt". "Take the dirt from the hill and spread it in the sun," he wrote. "Mix with milk letting the dirt wash away and leaving behind a juice. Dry it out and the result is sulfur."[10]

Still, Lu was not the first. The Chinese have been extracting sulfur for centuries. The earliest uses of the mineral were by Daoist alchemists attempting to melt gold or to concoct immortality elixirs. The result of com-bining sulfur with saltpeter produced neither. "If you mix together sulfur, realger, and saltpeter then ignite them, fire will spurt forth burning your hands, face, and even your house!" warned the Daoist book of chemical formulas dated somewhere around A.D. 850.

The book went on to list thirty-five dangerous elixirs, the concocting of which, it warned, could produce devastating results. Three of them involve the main ingredients of gunpowder.[11] However, some seven hundred years later the alchemists did take to treating the amalgam as a drug, as one sixteenth-century Daoist priest testified: "Gunpowder has a bitter-sour sapidity, and is slightly toxic. It can be used to treat sores and ringworm, it kills worms and insects, and it dispels damp and hot epidemic fevers."[12]

A most curious elixir, considering the highly toxic properties of sulfur. What the early wizards were after, it seems, was a method to refine the saltpeter which had supposedly given immense longevity to a second-century adept who ingested a quantity of it, or some other mineral of similar nature. This is an odd phenomenon as saltpeter is potassium nitrate, quantities of which will make someone ghastly sick in the same manner as ingesting salt water.

The Han Dynasty (206 B.C. - A.D. 220) certainly knew this and made laws in the beginning of the first century A.D. against extracting the mineral as well as mixing it with any other substances. "From the day of the summer solstice onwards strong fires are forbidden, as well as the smelting of metals with charcoal. The purification of saltpeter has to cease altogether, until the beginning of autumn..." read the Han legal code. The function of sulfur in gunpowder acts to lower saltpeter's ignition temperature to 250 degrees centigrade, and on combustion to increase the speed of fusion and raise the temperature to 335 degrees. Boom! Such a wonderful combination that John Bate commented, "the Saltpeter is the Soule, the Sulphur the Life, and the Coales the Body."[13]

This splendiferous Daoist invention found its way into the annuls of military institutions changing, as Roger Bacon reflected in 1620, "the whole face and state of things throughout the world."[14] In the tenth century the Chinese began packing the minerals into a bamboo tube giving birth to the first flame thrower. Crude albeit, but it did appositely burn the hands and face, and even the houses, of the enemy. By the end of that century Chinese inventors were making small bombs and grenades by stuffing the gunpowder into clay or wooden spheres. Given such practices the Chinese appropriately called the substance *huo yao*, or "fire medicine," in respect to its Daoist history.[15]

The Yuan Dynasty successfully put the fire medicine to practical use, expanding their kingdom throughout central Asia. Under Yuan occupation, the Arabs picked up on the secret substance and produced a complete text on gunpowder which they used to assault the Europeans in the forteenth-century wars. Hostilities aside, the Arabs sent two cannons to the French king in 1345 along with two hundred cannonballs and eight pounds of gun-powder. That same year the English, afraid that their continental counter-parts were making threatening advances in military science, commissioned the development of rocket propelled grenades.[16] These splendid inventions, Bacon noted,"disturb the hearing to such a degree that if they are set off suddenly at night with sufficient skill neither cities nor armies can endure them. No thunderclap can compare with such terrifying noises; nor light-ening playing among the clouds with such frightening flashes..."[17]

So the history of modern warfare planted its roots, evolving into military might that could lead nations to conquer and peoples to be destroyed; just, as Robert Boyle remarked,"as the poor Indians lookt upon the Spaniards as more than Men, because the knowledge they had of the properties of Nitre, Sulphur and Charcoale duly mixed, enabled them to Thunder and Lighten so fatelly, when they pleas'd."[18]   ☙

Yu also knows that he can thunder and lightning against his so-called savages. He knows that wars between the swarming and ever present European traders will erupt. He understands the importance of his sulfur extracting mission. With all of Chinese civilization and its glory riding on his shoulders, Yu knows he must not fail.

My servant is sick and for every ten workers, nine are ill. Even the cook is sick and there is no one to hold the wok. Wang has serious dysentery and cannot keep in water or liquid. Day and night he goes out seventy to eighty times [to relieve himself], but soon just lets it ooze out onto his pillow and mat. Sickness swarms at very corner of my bed; I hear moaning and shivering, like a concert that begins and doesn't stop.

YU YONGHE

病且殆乎

PART 9

Sickness and Death

臺灣圖

Detail of the Taiwan coast. A good illustration of the rivers Yu traveled across. From Haiguo Wenjian Lu, 1744.

Yu had a particular fear of Taiwan's snakes, especially after he saw one trying to swallow a deer. First published in Par M.J. Thomson's Voyage en Chine, *1870-1872.*

Sickness and Death

Yu wants to explore the mountains surrounding his camp. Setting out together with Gu, he hires an aborigine boat with two oarsmen to take them up river. They go to where the river ends at Upper Beitou and find a native to serve as a guide.

As they move into the woods they suddenly find themselves swallowed in saw grass over three meters high. The midday sun beats down on the top making it hot and stuffy below. Yu cannot breath. Gu has a knife and goes first, cutting a path so they can move easier through the field. But Yu falls behind by only five steps and loses Gu and the guide in the grass. He stops and listens to their rustling.

Within a kilometer they are out of the overgrown bush. They cross two streams and venture into a bigger forest with many trees and vines wrapped up the trees like a dragon attempting to strangle its prey. The wind blows leaves the size of Yu's hand to the ground. He finds new trees growing in the mud which are ten full arm lengths in diameter. Amongst them frolic birds that he cannot see but that make sounds he has never before heard.

They scale six hills and come to a large river some 15 meters wide. The blue-green water moving quietly over rocks interests Yu and the guide tells him it is a natural hot spring originating from sulfur deposits. Curious Yu scalds himself when he reaches out to touch the water. He uses a pole to help himself across.

After another kilometer there are no trees and Yu can see clearly the mountain in front of him. Scrambling up the slope, he can feel the heat from the rocks. "The grass here is yellow and unhealthy," and white smoke rises out of the mountainside like fog. Their guide says the fog is actually steam coming from sulfur pots. The wind blows it their direction repulsing Yu with the smell. Within a few hundred meters the vegetation does not grow at all. The ground is hot as though the rocks have caught fire. Yu sees over fifty pillars of steam rising out of the ground and mud bubbling. "This whole place is like a big pot, in which we are walking on the lid." A rock on the right has a huge hole in it. Yu climbs up to have a look, and when he does a "poison fire jumps out." He cannot see and his head feels as if it will explode. He runs back a hundred steps, where he slowly recovers from the excruciating heat and foul fumes.

The party returns on the same road they came in on. Yu cannot get the smell of sulfur out of his clothes, but he has found the river that sounds like a waterfall in the gorge. Off to the left, where the boiling spring comes from, a large river flows, the sound of its rapids echoing off the hills.

During a quiet night at camp, Yu sharpens his literary talents with a poem about the day's trip:

In May there are no visitors.
In the east lies a volcano,
and no one can seem to find the hot spring.
The rocks all have a crystal powder
and the sulfur darkens them like ink.
A bubbling noise reaches the ships at sea
but it is not the sound of the streams.

FOLLOWING WEEKS
YU'S CAMP, BEITOU

Yu now sees that the land and the water in the north can make people very sick. "After a while everything rots. Those that come die, and no one knows if it is from ghosts or poison," he says.

The dreaded sicknesses everyone warned of have finally caught up with Yu's party. "At first I did not believe them but my servant got sick and now nine out of ten people in our party are stricken." Even the cook has come down with something horrible and there is no one to prepare meals. When Wang returned from a walk down to the sea he almost died. He has serious dysentery and cannot even drink water. Everything he consumes comes out the other end. Yu has kept count and Wang is forced to squat in the woods eighty times a day. "Now he just stays in bed and lets it run all over his pillow and blankets."

Wang's suffering is not uncommon, as those in Taiwan Fu tried to warn. Although disease has afflicted 90 percent of Yu's party, the immigrants all understand the phenomenon. The saying goes that for every ten immigrants arriving in Taiwan six will die, three stay, and one return. Of those that stay all get sick within three months.[1] .

The Spanish found themselves deathly sick and confined to bed so that they could not man posts or carry out the many tasks of building and keeping up the fort. The Manila council noted that "many die because of the bad climate in this land."[2]

Commodore Pickering observed that the Taiwan people are "decimated by the deadly fever of the jungle,"[3] and missionary George Mackay called it "man's deadliest foe—malarial fever, honeycombing a man's system with poison." Mackay wrote that "the bacteria of Asiatic cholera and malarial fever, carried on the wind, sweep over the country like a deathful pestilence...because of it disease and death work terrible havoc among the inhabitants."[4]

Yu tries to make sense of it by reasoning that "the mountains, just like the plains, have no ghosts. People get sick in the mountains because of the lack of development, and the grass and trees obstruct the light. The air gets poisoned and if it goes into the lungs then you get sick. Everyone will get sick."

Yet strangely, Yu does not get sick. He is the only one from his party who does not suffer from some malady. "Sick people are all around me, I constantly hear them moaning." Yu wishes he were a doctor and could heal them but the "only thing I can do is put them on a ship home." He sends them back to Fujian under Gu's supervision. Only Yu and his sick servant remain in Danshui. "I am the only one who is not sick," he writes. "Should this make me proud?"

It is a wonder Yu does not get sick. He supervises the aborigines collecting dirt and extracting sulfur. Everyday he is out under the hot sun with no time to rest. The sun burns his back and head. He must use his every resource to try to communicate with the aborigines, because "I don't speak their language and they can't understand what I say." Yu says he feels like a "deaf and dumb idiot." He knows his body is in bad shape. "Over the past ten years I have often fallen ill and must eat medicine as if it were food."

At fifty years old, Yu is reaching his senior years. Chinese officials rarely had strong, robust physiques. Having to devote all of their time to the study and memorization of the classic texts, they were skinny and frail. Few lived beyond sixty, and many died in their late fifties. Most shunned exercise and adventure. In this regard Yu is unique. Yet Yu also knows that peasants only live to forty or fifty years old, and they spend their whole lives outside walking and toiling under the sun. Yu worries that even if he makes it out of here alive, his days of natural life may be numbered.

The insects have also begun to torment Yu. "Billions of flying bugs rush at me like rain falling. Even my clothes do not stop them from setting about and biting my whole body." The mosquitoes, flies and leeches "suck my blood like they are hungry eagles and tigers. I cannot keep them off me." He notes that leeches "climb up the trees and hide in the leaves. When people walk underneath they fall like rain, on your head and neck, wiggling down into your clothes." If they come from the ground, they crawl up your legs. "They suck your blood and crawl all over your skin. So many that you can't pull them all off your body!"⁵ Those that hear of the leeches in the north turn purple and fear them more than tigers. Yu says the government and settlers have previously tried to burn the jungle to rid it of the dreaded leeches but everything is too wet and will not catch fire.

The snakes torment him too. "I am afraid of snakes," he says. At night the cobras scream, sometimes loud enough to scare the oxen. Yu has seen a snake "swallowing a deer so big that it could not get the hooves down its throat. " The small ones are just as bad, for they will chase people. One night the cook went outside and ran into a snake as big around as a cooking pan. After that incident everyone stopped going outside after dark.

Alone and stuck in the hostile jungle, Yu feels like he is on another planet. His house is made of grass, which lets the wind blow in from all four directions. "My bed has become a lawn, with grass growing from it, and when I pull it out it just grows back." When it rains, Yu's house has a river running through the front door. Even when it stops he must sleep in a hammock for ten days before his bed dries. When the river swells, the water comes right up to Yu's front door.

When the season is dry, the grass takes over the task of drowning of a person. It grows high over a man's head, and even at its shortest height it comes up to Yu's shoulders. The sharp jagged edges "will cut my face and neck." The trees get so overgrown, twisting upon each other, that Yu "can't even begin to explain their incestuous intricacies." The "evil bamboo" keeps him from seeing anything, though he hears the ocean howling at night. "The forest is full of sounds that howl. So much howling that my roof will cave in." The monkeys join the furor, "crying like ghosts as the candles flicker."

The aborigines have already shown their hostility. The night Yu arrived in Danshui a fisherman was building a house at the south end of the lake. The lone fisherman slept outside beneath the stars. In the middle of the night arrows flew and made twenty-eight holes in the man's pillow case. "I thought I was dreaming," Yu says. Another arrow flew and hit the fisherman in the arm. That night other aborigines were killed on the path by the same type of arrows. "I live in a place with no people, yet see aborigines running around. How can I not live in fear of their arrows?"

These are the raw aborigines, the ones that the government cannot control. "They often creep down from the hills and steal things, kill people, burn houses, then run back," Yu says. If these aborigines take victims they sever the heads and take them back to cook into what Missionary Reverend William Campbell termed "human brain cakes" and "brain-glue tablets." Campbell wrote of how the aborigines "boil down every head brought in to a thick jelly, from which thin oblong cakes are made, for being nibbled to inspire fresh courage."[6] Campbell once ran into a carefree lad with "two freshly cut Chinamen's heads which he had fastened by the queues over his shoulder." The aborigine boy let the heads serve as a pillow.[7]

Apart from using the heads as a sleeping accessory, the aborigines dress up the skulls with paint and line them up in front of their doors. "Whoever has the most skulls is considered the bravest," Yu says. The warriors hide in the grass and attack settlers wandering out alone; they sneak up behind them and plunge a knife into their skull. The Spanish said the Danshui natives "would hide along the path of the river and shoot arrows to kill and then cut the heads." Yu warns that "like a tiger that will eat you if you cross its path, or a snake that will bite, it is better to just leave them alone. If you stay away from their nest they will not attack you."

Under such conditions and with such depression hanging over him, Yu wants to give up. "I don't have a body of rock. I am weaker than the smallest mouse and at fifty years old my hair is gray. I have a mother still alive. How can I remain in such a dangerous place?" He says that "no one in the world is suffering more than I right now." He quotes poet Liu Zihou: "Buozhou is not a place for people." But, Yu says, "If Liu knew of this place where I am now he would think Buozhou heaven."

He tells himself that he must pull himself through this misery. He tries to reaffirm his stubborn and strong will. "In this life I have run into my share of problems; this is not the first time. My work here is not finished. Who else will finish it? If I leave today then I might as well not have come in the first place." He tells himself not to be afraid, he reminds himself that adventure includes danger and that the two complement each other. "I must decide to stay and reassert my will. I cannot let these frightening mountains and ghosts defeat me."

Darkness descends upon Yu in his lone and nearly deserted camp; the monkeys take up their racket. A damp drizzle bleeds out of the evening fog.

SEPTEMBER 1, THE GHOST FESTIVAL
YU'S CAMP, BEITOU

Twelve new workers have arrived from Fujian. Yu cooks a big meal and they eat together. Afterwards they all face the mountain and pray to put the ghosts at ease. Yu gives the workers wine to drink.

SEPTEMBER 4
YU'S CAMP, BEITOU

The ghosts have not been pleased. The workers have fallen ghastly ill and a strong wind blows out of the north. Twelve of the invalids cannot get out of bed. The camp is deathly void of human activity. Smoke does not even rise from the cooking fire.

A strong wind begins to blow out of the north.

Strong wind is called 'ty' and the ty has no set schedule but it will certainly come with heavy rains; it will uproot trees and blow down fences and carry away roof tiles and break rocks. The longer time passes without one, the stronger it is when it comes. Even if ships are anchored they will be broken up into planks.

YU YONGHE

颱
風

PART 10

Typhoon

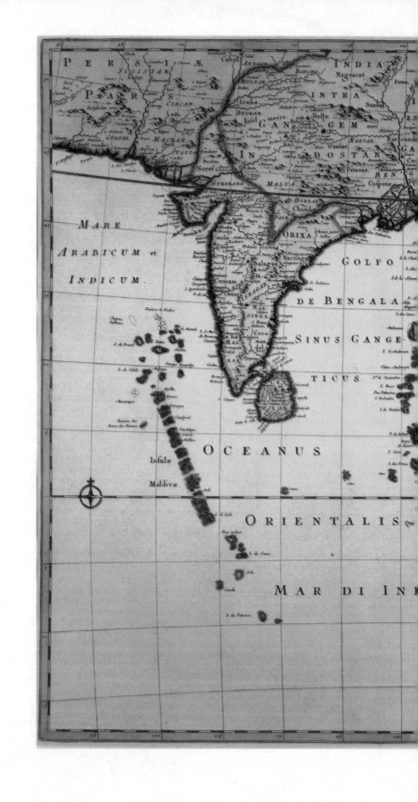

Dutch detail of South East Asia. By Fredrick De Wit, 1662.

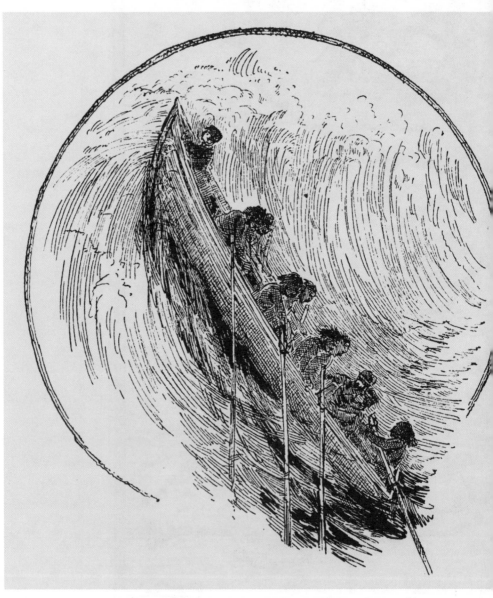
Caught at sea in a typhoon. Captain Lindsay Anderson, 1891.

Typhoon

SEPTEMBER 4

YU'S CAMP, BEITOU

For three days and nights the wind does not rest. It pulls the trees out of the ground and blows away half of the camp's houses. Yu cannot sleep at night. "I hear the crashing of trees and the roaring of waves ringing in my ear. There is a hole in the roof where water pours down like stream. I wake up many times throughout the night. I cannot press my eyelids together."

SEPTEMBER 7

DANSHUI HILLS

The torrents of rain increase and the strength of the wind grows. The grass roof veranda in front of Yu's house gets blown away like a butterfly floating in the breeze. The thick bamboo stalks in the camp break and Yu fears his house will succumb to the wind and rain. He runs out with a hat and axe to cut wood and reinforce his house. He fells six trees to serve as pillars for his sagging roof. "I have no strength left."

Like dry leaves cast into a raging river, the mountain has begun to throw its dirt and trees downwards. Streams cut through the forest, fighting gravity to fall faster and bring everything down with them. Mud comes off the hill as if it were alive and hoped to smother the lakeside in a suffocating embrace.

Yu calls the canoes to take the sick people down to Danshui Village. He runs back to see if he can save the houses but the water has already swallowed them. He scrambles to the grass plain above the houses but the water chases him there too. As he sits thinking of where he may be safe, the water swells around his ankles, up to his waist, and now Yu is swimming, the water clawing at his neck.

He walks two kilometers through the mud, water and wind. The strength of the gusts blow him over. He gets back up and climbs upward out of the basin to an aborigine village. Yu can finally rest, tired but hungry. "I trade my clothes for a live chicken to feed my unforgiving stomach."

The wind howls all night.

SEPTEMBER 8
DANSHUI

By morning the wind and rain have stopped. And by noon a hint of sunshine threatens to poke through the clouds. Yu takes an aborigine canoe down the mountain. He passes the spot where his camp once stood. Now a field of mud covers his houses and sulfur extraction factory. Everything is gone and Yu is lucky to be alive.

He sails down to Danshui where he gives his remaining clothes, which are dirty and torn, to a sailor to wash and dry in the sun. He stays on an anchored ship in the Danshui harbor.

SEPTEMBER 10

DANSHUI

The water levels have dropped. Yu rows out of the harbor to Big Zhang's house. With him he carries a man who has died from sickness, the first under Yu's care.

"He has died here and the body has no reason to travel back across the sea," Yu writes. He takes the dead man inland and buries him at the foot of the mountain.

SEPTEMBER 13

DANSHUI

The other sick patients on the boat are getting worse. Yu orders the ship to sail for Fujian.

Yu remains in Danshui, and will stay with Big Zhang until new houses can be built and another camp established.

SEPTEMBER 14

ARLING MOUNTAIN

The tempest has returned. For four days and nights the wind and rain punish the north of the island. Flood waters rush down from the hills once again.

Having witnessed the power of a typhoon just days before, and now "more afraid than the first time," Yu climbs out of the Danshui basin up to Arling Mountain. Although he has avoided the floodwaters and feels lucky to have left early, he is trapped on the mountain for a day and a night with nothing to eat.

Typhoon season will not let the island's inhabitants rest. Yu notes that every year Taiwan will be terrorized by typhoons, "sometimes earlier, sometimes later, but they will always come." When they do come, they uproot trees and set off landslides, blow away houses and bring down mountains. "People on the coast are most afraid of typhoons," Yu says. No wonder, for the waves they bring can drown harbors and sink boats.[1]

Taiwan's aborigines have long observed the natural menace of severe tropical storms. They say that when the rainbow is severed in half, a typhoon will certainly come. They say the Typhoon Grass can predict how many typhoons will hit the island that year. If one new segment of the grass grows then that year will see one typhoon, if two segments then two typhoons, and so forth. "Not once has this method proved incorrect," says the *Taiwan Fu Gazetteer*.[2]

The Chinese however, do not have as much experience with typhoons. Not until the seventeenth century did the word make its way into Chinese records. This is not to say that all of China had no such natural phenomena, but rather that northern China, where the compilers of history sat, has neve been prone to typhoons. Not until higher officials began traveling to the south do records of the heavy wind and rains begin. Some have even romanticized the connection of names between Taiwan and the typhoons that dance around the island. The *Taiwan Gazetteer* in the mid-eighteenth century said that the "Tai" of "Taiwan" and the "ty" of "typhoon" have the same pronunciation, "just add a wind radical to it and it becomes "ty" as in "typhoon." All books call it such."[3]

It was a defense report of 1625 that first used this "ty" character. In an investigation of Penghu the report said that "the four corners are all flat with no mountains to protect it. Typhoons and cyclones blow about."[4] Years later, the *Taiwan Fu Gazetteer* set about to explain the differences between a twister and this new phenomena of typhoon, saying that "when the winds are strong and blow like mad it is a cyclone (ju), when they are even stronger it is a typhoon (tai). Cyclones happen suddenly, while typhoons build up slowly. Cyclones cease abruptly, while typhoons drag on day and night for days at a time." Accordingly, cyclones occur during the first four months of the year, while typhoons strike from the fifth through the eighth months. "If a ship runs into a cyclone it can still sail but if it hits a typhoon it can do nothing."[5]

SEPTEMBER 22
DANSHUI

Yu has come down from the mountain and returned to Big Zhang's. A ship has arrived. Those on board say that three days prior three ships set sail from Fujian and ran into the typhoon. One capsized and one has been lost at sea.

Yu's friend Gu is on the missing ship. Yu is worried about Gu and everyday he goes down to the harbor to watch for his ship.

SEPTEMBER 29
THE MOON FESTIVAL

There are no moon cakes today. Two of the sick cannot return to Fujian because the ship has not come. They walk down to the beach with Yu to look and wait for its arrival. At noon Big Zhang brings lunch and the four of them picnic on the beach, drinking wine and trying to forget their pains and sufferings, trying to forget just where they are.

SEPTEMBER 30
YU'S CAMP, BEITOU

The new houses are finished. Yu takes an aborigine canoe upriver to the new camp. He brings the two sick men. The sick sleep together in one room. Yu has his own room, his own space, his own loneliness. "At night only a solitary shadow cast about the room." At night the monkeys still scream like banshees.

Yu occupies himself in the dark. He reads poetry by the former Taiwan

Fu magistrate Li Zigu by candlelight. One of these late sleepless nights, under the company of Li's characters, Yu is startled by a glowing light the size of a wash pan in front of his bed. It hovers some three feet off the ground. "I would be scared of ghosts but I know it is phosphorous. I sit and watch it for a long time, then it disappears."

OCTOBER 9
DANSHUI

A ship has arrived at the Danshui harbor. Yu rushes downriver from his camp to greet it.

It is Gu, he has been found.

"Where did the wind take you?" Yu asks.

"The day we set sail, there was no wind on the western coast. About halfway across the strait the wind suddenly picked up and the sailors struggled to control the ship. We saw Jilung and Arling Mountain, but the low tide kept us from being able to enter the harbor. A ship under the command of captain Chen tried and was smashed into the coast and sunk; so we turned the rudder and tried to head back to the western shore. We dropped anchor near an island. All the ship's instruments were broken or lost and needed to be replaced, and furthermore the strength of the wind was growing, and would continue to blow for half a month.

"We have come late, but at least we have arrived uninjured," Gu says.

"And what of the other junk, how are the sick workers who returned?" Yu asks.

"Over half have already died," Gu says.

Gu's ship has brought sixty workers to help with sulfur extraction. Within a month they too will be sick and dying.

At night, before the comfort of a fire in their camp, Yu and Gu reflect on this hostile world where they find themselves: a world of wild animals and mysterious sickness and stalking death. "This is not a world for people," Yu says. And yet, tonight, when all is well, Yu finds a masochistic pleasure in his mission. "Most people cannot endure this type of suffering," he tells Gu, "but we would not change our fate nor sacrifice this joy."

Yu climbs into bed but cannot sleep. Outside a glowing flame the size of a wash pan appears again. It burns the eyes. Gu asks why Yu has lit his candle. "That fire is from the side of your bed casting its light into my room. If you turn around you will certainly see it." Gu springs out of bed, puts on his clothes and rushes outside, but the phosphorus has already gone out.

OCTOBER 10
YU'S CAMP, BEITOU

Night. Yu hears rustling outside and fears the raw aborigines have come to terrorize him. He runs outside but sees nothing.

Before, I always wanted to go overseas to travel. I thought that I would taste the waters of the earth's seas and touch the highest mountains. Today I have already seen all the scenery and walked through unknown dangers. The so-called immortals are really naked peoples with tattoos all over their bodies!

YU YONGHE

FU CHEU FU ou HO...
tir...

A. { Fauxbourg de Lamth...
    Voorsteden van

B. { Pont de Trente Six ...
    Brug van zes-ender...

D

J. v. Schley direx.

Carving of Fuzhou, from the second Dutch embassy to China, 1662.
Nantai Bridge is on the right.

Believed to be the first European map of China. By Van der Broecke, 1584.
The map is orientated east.

eturn

NOVEMBER 14

YU'S CAMP, BEITOU

The sulfur extraction is complete. Yu has been busy over the past month rushing to make up the time he lost due to outbreaks of sickness and typhoons. He has worked hard and tried to keep the workers from falling ill again. Yu has been too busy to write much over the past month. Now, he writes that he is preparing to return to Fujian. He sends the workers to gather wood in the hills.

At noon Yu sends the rest of the party down to the coast to wait for the ship. He walks alone through the deserted camp. Spying four people sitting in a nearby tree he thinks the workers have returned early from their wood chopping expedition. He approaches the tree to ask them but when he looks up again he sees no one. Yu fears he is being haunted. "To live here it is hard enough not to get sick and die, no less to avoid the ghosts stalking you."

NOVEMBER 17

DANSHUI HARBOR

Yu is prepared to sail. He bids Big Zhang farewell and boards the ship.

Fort Zeelandia on "Taiouang." The earliest picture of the Dutch fort on Taiwan. From Seygert van Regteren's 1635 Version of Cadidius Account of the Island.

NAMING TAIWAN

There is one last thing before Yu leaves the island, and that is an explanation of its name. In the late seventeenth century, the island had two names, a European name and a Chinese name.

The Europeans called the island Formosa, and continued to call it that deep into the twentieth century. It was actually the first name given to the island; bestowed by the Portuguese, whose ships coasted along its shores in the mid-1540s. Observing the green mountains and magnificent cliffs, they called it Ilha Formosa, or Beautiful Isle. The name was first put on paper on a map drawn in 1554 by Portuguese cartographer Lopo Homem. He labeled the islands south of Japan "I. Fremoza".

But not until the 1580s was the name immortalized by a Dutchman, Jan Huyghen van Linschoten, then acting as the secretary to the Portuguese Archbishop of Goa, India. Linschoten interviewed Portuguese captains returning from voyages all over the world, and compiled all they told him in his Itinerario. This monumental work aimed to do nothing less than gather full descriptions of "all the courses, Havens, islands, depths, shallowes, sands, droughts, riffes and cliffs, with their situations, also the times of the yeares when the winds blow, with the true tokens and knowledge of the tides and the weather, water, and streams in all the Orientall coasts and Havens, as they are observed and set downe by the Kings Pilots, in their continuall and dayly Voyages."[1] Towards the end of this voluminous work, Formosa was named, and later that century, the name found its way into the dictionary, so that the Western world, for centuries after, would come to know the island as Formosa.

That was long before anyone formally called the island Taiwan. Immigrants of the late sixteenth century might have used the two characters *Mai Yuan*—"mai," meaning bury, and "yuan," unjust—to refer to a far off land in which disasters have caused the early death of many. In the Southern Fujian dialect, the characters are pronounced *Dai Wan*.[2] But in Taiwan's early years, no one in China cared much for the island and certainly not enough to write down a name. Government officials still used an ambiguous Liuqiu to refer to either Taiwan or any of the islands along the Pacific rim. So it was from the spoken word that different written forms arose in the early seventeenth century. Chen Di, in his short work *Records on the Eastern Savages*, wrote that "the place where the eastern savages live is called Dayuan*."[3] A few years later a work on the surrounding seas used similar characters to refer to Taiwan. Both names are pronounced as Dai Wan in the Southern Fujian dialect.

It took the impetus of a colonizer, however, before the name "Taiwan" would come into widespread use. When the Dutch came to Taiwan Fu in the 1620s they heard the locals pronouncing *Daiwan*, which was translated for them as *Da Wan*, or great bay. They thus took to calling the area the "Groote baye," or "Tayouan," while the island as a whole remained as Formosa.[4] This can be seen from the following Dutch sailing record of 1623: "we set sail for Tayouan...In the morning we saw Isla Formosa and made port

---

* 大員

in the bay of Tayouan."[5] Although the Zhengs discarded the name in favor of Dongning, use of the spoken word continued. When the Qing arrived in the 1680s, they drew up the characters *Tai* and *Wan**, bestowing it with the name that it would carry into the present day.[6]

Detail of the first western map to label Taiwan, here labeled as I. Fremoza.
Lopo Homem, 1554.

---

* 臺灣

NOVEMBER 20

IN THE TAIWAN STRAIT

After three days of calm seas and no breeze, the winds finally begin to pick up. In the mid-afternoon, Yu's ship is the first to sail out of Danshui harbor, followed by Gu's. The north wind grows stronger and the rough seas soon begin to toss the ships about.

Taiwan has not even dropped over the horizon when the thunderous sound of wood breaking echoes across the sea. The wind has snapped his ship's mast. Yu looks back just in time to see the mast on Gu's ship also crash into the ocean.

Unable to return to Danshui they have no choice but to let the north wind carry them where it will.

Yu has begun to panic beyond all reason. "We will float thousands of li down past Taiwan and into the southern seas."

He cannot sleep at night.

NOVEMBER 21

GUANTANG ISLANDS

The wind has stopped. The night's mist has not yet disappeared from the water as dawn breaks over the aft of the ship, a red sun bobbing on the horizon, three times disappearing and reappearing behind the rocking boat. The calm sea sparkles and turns orange as a ball the size of cartwheel lifts into the sky. Yu is already dressed and on deck for the spectacle. "I have heard the sunrise in Dengzhou is incredible but it could not compare to this."

The dawn's glory has calmed Yu's spirits and he is relieved to see mountains frolicking in the mist on the western horizon. The captain says they are approaching the Gauntang Islands.*

---

* An early name for the Mazu Islands.

Although the north wind blew them out into the strait and possibly far south, the currents running from south to north have over compensated for their loss of latitude. When the wind stopped blowing sometime in early morning, Yu's ship rode the southern currents to the northern coast of Fujian. At midnight they reach the Guantang Islands, a small cluster of habitable islands just a few kilometers off the Fujian coast.

NOVEMBER 22

FUJIAN COAST

Yu spots Gu's ship as they approach Dinghai Township on the Fujian coast. Gu has already arrived in Dinghai, but Yu cannot believe he has arrived at all, nor himself for that matter. Like some surreal dream from which he has just peacefully emerged, Yu can find no sound reason why they should both be safe. "After the masts broke I though we would never make it back to Fujian," Yu writes. "Praise the gods for their help."

The ships travel another 30 kilometers down the coast to Wuhu-men,* the gate to Fuzhou. Here two rocks check all travel further into the inlet. They create a tight crevice from which access up to the city of Fuzhou can be blocked. Here a chain of rocks descends into the sea like five tigers squatting in the current, standing guard over the door to Fujian province.

Outside the door, a powerful wind blows in off the sea. It almost flips over Yu's ship. But once they pass through the crevice, everything is calm. Like a quiet lake, the channel leading up to Fuzhou is starkly different from the angry sea outside the door.

The ships move upstream towards Fuzhou. They still have at least a day's journey if the winds are favorable, or more if they are not.

Instead of pressing onwards, the captain stops in Tingtou, a large

* Literally, Five Tiger Gate.

fishing village on the channel for the night. Eager to get off the boat, Yu and Gu go to the Yishan Monastery where they engage the monks in discussion before bedding down.

NOVEMBER 25

FUZHOU

Yu can see Fuzhou's Nantai Bridge! For the past two days the wind has been dead and the ship has been unable to sail the last few kilometers up river. With his home so close, Yu began to chafe, hastily writing that "we can't even move a mile." Growing overly anxious, Yu commanded the sailors to man the scull and get them home.

Yu's friend Zhou Xuanyu comes to greet him with a landing skiff, and Yu hopes that his other friends will be there too when he gets to shore.

He is sorely disappointed. No one is in Fuzhou. In the past ten months, when Yu was away, his friends have gradually disappeared from the city. Some have returned to their homes in other cities and provinces and some have drifted off to other areas. Yu feels very alone now.

He walks around the city that was once so familiar but now seems a world away. Yu feels that he has returned from a different era, a different world, a different life. Everything is so close, and yet so far away, as if he cannot quite adjust to life back in the bustling cities of China, where the merchants hawk and haggle and everyone is so suspicious of each other. A life where the bureaucracy is so close, close enough to define existence, and where his friends have all gone away.

As a last reflection Yu writes: "I look at the city and I can't help but think of where I have lived over the past year. I can't help but be haunted by that land where no one lives. I feel as if I have gone off and died somewhere, and now return to this world as a crane."[*]

---

[*] Yu is referring to the mythical tale of Ding Lingwei who died and came back as a crane because he wanted to see his home once again.

But it is a land from which Yu has just emerged, a land which few in China know anything about. It is a land on which Yu must write.

> I have traveled to distant shores,
> and to far away lands where men do not venture.
> I have been to the heights of the mountains
> and the depths of the rivers,
> I have escaped death
> from the island's most cunning dangers.
> I have lived the lives of the savages,
> I have walked through it all;
> how can I not leave word to let the rest of the world know.[7]

NOTES

I have used Fang Hao's edition of Yu Yonghe's *Pihai Jiyou*. Unless specified, all quotes and passages pertaining to Yu and his journey correspond to the same date in the Chinese text. The quotes at the beginning of each chapter are not numbered but refered to with "QUOTE."

PROLOGUE (pp. 1-9)

QUOTE: 郁永河，《裨海紀遊》（臺北市：臺灣銀行經濟研究室, 1957-61），卷上，頁 14.

1. 福建通志局，《福建通紀》（台北市：大通書局，1968），卷 14。

2. 盧之頤，《本草乘雅半偈》，清順治丁亥(四年)錢塘盧氏月樞閣刊本（台北市：國立中央圖書館縮影室，1981）。

3. Fr. Jacinto Esquivel, 1632, *in* Jose Eugenio Borao Mateo, ed., *Spaniards in Taiwan. Vol. I: 1582-1641*, (Taipei, 2001), 168.

4. 7 October 1642, VOC 1140, (1643III), ff. 306-307, *in* Jose Eugenio Borao Mateo, ed., *Spaniards in Taiwan* Vol. II: 1642-1682 (Taipei, 2002), 393.

5. *See* 史明，《台灣人四百年史》（草根文化出版社，1998），頁 140；John Robert Shepherd, *Statecraft and Political Economy on the Taiwan Frontier: 1600-1800* (Stanford, 1993), 144.

6. 郁永河，《裨海紀遊》（臺北市：臺灣銀行經濟研究室, 1957-61），卷上，1。

7. 郁永河，《裨海紀遊》（臺北市：臺灣銀行經濟研究室, 1957-61），卷上，1。

8. Quote from, 清世宗敕編，《聖祖仁皇帝聖訓》，卷 50。

9. See, 陳第，〈東番記〉，*in* 沈有容，《閩海贈言》（臺北市：臺灣銀行經濟研究室 1959），卷 2。

10. 連雅堂，《臺灣通史》（臺北市：臺灣銀行經濟研究室, 1957-61），卷 30〈列傳〉2。

PART 1 (pp. 10-31)

QUOTE: 郁永河，《裨海紀遊》（臺北市：臺灣銀行經濟研究室, 1957-61），卷上，頁 9.

1. *See* 郁永河，《裨海紀遊》（臺北市：臺灣銀行經濟研究室, 1957-61），卷中，頁 17。

2. For descriptions of Qing troops and weaponry see, 《兵不可一日不備—清代軍事文獻特展導覽手冊》[*Eternal Vigilance: Special Exhibition of Ching Military Documents*]（國立故宮博物院，2002）。

3. Date and scene from 郁永河,《裨海紀遊》, 卷上, 頁 3。

4. *See* 諸家,《清耆獻類徵選編》(臺北市：臺灣銀行經濟研究室, 1967), 卷 6。

5. 清世宗敕編, 《聖祖仁皇帝庭訓格言》, 卷 64; *see also* Jonathan D. Spence, *Emperor of China* (New York, 1988), 35.

6. 江日昇,《臺灣外記》(臺北市：臺灣銀行經濟研究室, 1957-1961), 卷 9, 頁 415。

7. 江日昇,《臺灣外記》(臺北市：臺灣銀行經濟研究室, 1957-61), 卷 10, 頁 440; 施琅, 〈飛報大捷疏〉, *in*《靖海紀事》(臺北市：臺灣銀行經濟研究室, 1957-61), 卷上, 頁 28。

8. Dialogue from, 江日昇,《臺灣外記》(臺北市：臺灣銀行經濟研究室, 1957-61), 卷 9, 頁 416。

9. 施琅, 〈飛報大捷疏〉, *in*《靖海紀事》(臺北市：臺灣銀行經濟研究室, 1957-61), 卷上, 頁 29; *see also* Pei-kai Cheng, *et al.*, *The Search for Modern China, a Documentary Collection* (New York, 1999), 48-51.

10. 諸家,《清耆獻類徵選編》(臺北市：臺灣銀行經濟研究室, 1967), 卷 6, 頁 551。

11. 諸家,《清耆獻類徵選編》(臺北市：臺灣銀行經濟研究室, 1967), 卷 6, 頁 568。

12. 郁永河,《裨海紀遊》(臺北市：臺灣銀行經濟研究室, 1957-61), 卷下。

13. 郁永河,《裨海紀遊》(臺北市：臺灣銀行經濟研究室, 1957-61), 卷上。

14. *See The English Factory in Taiwan : 1670-1685* (Taipei, 1995).

15. 江日昇,《臺灣外記》(臺北市：臺灣銀行經濟研究室, 1957-61), 卷 6; 黃宗羲, 〈鄭成功傳〉, *in*《賜姓始末》(臺北市：臺灣銀行經濟研究室, 1957-61), 頁 61。

16. 郁永河, 〈鄭氏逸事〉, *in*《裨海紀遊》(臺北市：臺灣銀行經濟研究室, 1957-61), 頁 47。

17. 張煌言, 〈上延平王書〉, *in*《張蒼水詩文集》(臺北市：臺灣銀行經濟研究室, 1962), 〈冰槎集〉, 頁 30。

18. *Quoted in* C. Imbault-Huart, *L'ile Formose, Histoire et Description* (Paris, 1893), 52.

19. 郁永河, 〈鄭氏逸事〉, *in*《裨海紀遊》(臺北市：臺灣銀行經濟研究室, 1957-61), 頁 49。

20. Juan Ferrando, *Historia de los PP Dominicos, Vol. III* (Madrid, 1871), 65-66, *quoted in* Donald Keene, *The Battles of Coxinga, Chikamatsu's Puppet Play, its Background and Importance* (Cambridge, 1971), 52.

21. *Quoted in* C. Imbault-Huart, *L'ile Formosa, Histoire et Description* (Paris, 1893), 52.

22. C.E.S., Verwaarloosde Formosa, *in* WM. Campbell, *Formosa Under the Dutch* (London, 1903), 384.

23. 莊金德,〈鄭氏軍糧問題的研討——從鄭氏的缺糧徵糧到屯田臺灣〉, *in* 《臺灣文獻》,卷 12 期 1, 頁 437。

24. C.E.S., Verwaarloosde Formosa, *in* WM. Campbell, *Formosa Under the Dutch* (London, 1903), 407.

PART 2 (pp. 32-57)

QUOTE: 黃榮洛,〈勸君切莫過台灣——「渡台悲歌」的發現研究〉, *in*《渡臺悲歌：台灣的開拓與抗爭史話》(台北市：臺原出版社, 1989) 頁 24。

1. Interviews with Penghu fishermen, Magung, Pier 1, May 2002.

2. Interviews with ROC Navy Captain, April 2002.

3. For instance, *see* 謝金鑾,《續修臺灣縣志》(臺北市：臺灣銀行經濟研究室, 1962),卷 1〈地志：海道〉,頁 30。

4. 黃榮洛,〈勸君切莫過台灣——「渡台悲歌」的發現研究〉, *in*《渡臺悲歌：台灣的開拓與抗爭史話》(台北市：臺原出版社, 1989), 頁 24。

5. Interviews with Penghu fishermen, Magung Pier 1, May 2002.

6. *See* 黃富三, 〈清代台灣之移民的耕地取得問題及其對土著的影響上〉, *in* 《食貨》, 卷 11 期 1, 頁 22; 湯熙勇,〈近世環中國海的海難資料集介紹〉, *in*《漢學研究通訊》, 卷 19 期 1(1990 年 2 月), 頁 141。

7. 唐羽,〈清代渡台漳泉移民制度之研究〉, in《契約文書與社會生活—臺灣與華南社會(1600-1900)》研討會論文(1999.3)。

8. 陳文達,《臺灣縣志》(臺北市：臺灣銀行經濟研究室, 1957-61)。

9. 藍鼎元的詩, *in* 朱仕玠,《小琉球漫誌》(臺北市：臺灣銀行經濟研究室, 1957-61),卷 7, 頁 75。

10. Franois Valentyn, *quoted in* WM. Campbell, *Formosa Under the Dutch* (London, 1903), 26.

11. *Quoted in* Hsu Wen-hsiung, Aboriginal Island to Chinese Frontier. *In China's Island Frontier*, Ronald G. Knapp, ed. (Hawaii 1980), 12.

12. *Quoted in* Leonard Blusse, 'Another Voice from the Past: the Dutch occupation of Peng-hu and the first Dutch settlement on Taiwan, between Myth and Reality' (paper presented at *The International Symposium on the Image of Taiwan During the Dutch Period*, Oct. 14, 2001), 56.

13. *Quoted in* 史明,《台灣人四百年史》(San Jose, 1980), 57, 72; *see also* WM. Campbell, *Formosa Under the Dutch* (London, 1903), 31.

14. WM. Campbell, *Formosa Under the Dutch* (London, 1903), 30-35.

15. *Quoted in* Leonard Blusse, Natalie Everts and Evelien Frech, ed., *The Formosan Encounter: Notes on Formosa's Aboriginal Society: A Selection of Documents from Dutch Archival Sources, Vol I: 1623-1635* (Taipei, 1999), xiii; WM. Campbell, *Formosa Under the Dutch* (London, 1903), 27.

16. *Quoted in* C.R. Boxer, *The Rise and Fall of Nicholas Iquan, in Tian Hsia Monthly*, 11(5):412 (April-May 1941).

17. *Quoted in* Lo-shu Fu, *A Documentary Chronicle of Sino-Western Relations*, 1644-1820 (University of Arizona, 1966), 59.

18. Descriptions from, 高拱乾, 《臺灣府志》（臺北市：臺灣銀行經濟研究室, 1960）, 卷 1〈封域志〉, 頁7; 陳文達等編纂, 《鳳山縣志》（臺北市：臺灣銀行經濟研究室, 1961）, 卷 2〈規制志〉, 頁 33。

19. 道光 6 年 5 月, 觀喜, 〈爲內閣抄出閩浙總督兼署福建巡撫孫爾準奏〉, *in* 《臺案彙錄丁集》（臺北市：臺灣銀行經濟研究室, 1963）, 卷 2, 頁 146。

20. WM. Campbell, *Formosa Under the Dutch* (London, 1903), 27.

21. 高拱乾, 《臺灣府志》（臺北市：臺灣銀行經濟研究室, 1960）, 卷 2〈規制志〉, 頁 51。

22. 江日昇, 《臺灣外記》（臺北市：臺灣銀行經濟研究室, 1957-61）, 卷 5, 頁 194。

23. C.E.S., Verwaarloosde Formosa, *in* WM. Campbell, *Formosa Under the Dutch* (London, 1903), 412-418.

24. *See* 郁永河, 〈海上紀略〉, *in*《裨海紀遊》（臺北市：臺灣銀行經濟研究室, 1957-61）, 頁 60。

25. 川口長孺, 《臺灣鄭氏紀事》, （臺北市：臺灣銀行經濟研究室, 1958）, 卷之中, 頁 48。

26. *See* WM. Campbell, *Formosa Under the Dutch* (London, 1903), 63-64, 328, 386, 388, 398-9, 410-427, 456, 459, 460.

PART 3 (pp. 58-81)

QUOTE: 施琅, 〈恭陳台灣棄留疏〉, *in*《靖海紀事》, （臺北市：臺灣銀行經濟研究室, 1957-61）, 下卷, 頁 59。

1. Missive, Pieter Jansz Muyser, Tayouan, 4 November 1624, VOC 1083, fol. 510-511, *in* Leonard Blusse, Natalie Everts and Evelien Frech, ed., *The Formosan Encounter: Notes on Formosa's Aboriginal Society: A Selection of Documents from Dutch Archival Sources, Vol. I: 1623-1635* (Taipei, 1999), 33.

2. 高拱乾,《臺灣府志》(台北市:臺灣銀行經濟研究室, 1960), 卷 7〈風土志〉, 189。

3. 趙孟頫,《松雪齋文集》, 卷 4, *quoted in* 賴福順,〈發現台灣: 兼述中國文獻與「台灣論」〉(未出版), 頁 53。

4. *See* 賴福順,〈發現台灣:兼述中國文獻與「台灣論」〉(未出版), 頁 52-54。

5. 明太祖撰,《皇明祖訓》, *Quoted in* 賴福順,〈探索元明時期中國與小琉球國的關係: 兼述朱元璋與「兩國論」〉, *in*《中國現代史專題研究報告》, 第 22 輯(中華民國史料研究中心, 2001)頁 57-172。

6. 覺羅勒德洪奉敕撰,《大清聖祖仁(康熙)皇帝實錄》, 卷 111; *see also* Lo-shu Fu, *A Documentary Chronicle of Sino-Western Relations, 1644-1820* (University of Arizona, 1966), 60.

7. 施琅,〈恭陳台灣棄留疏〉, *in*《靖海紀事》(臺北市:臺灣銀行經濟研究室, 1957-61), 卷下, 頁 60。

8. *See* M. Paske-Smith, *Western Barbarians in Japan and Formosa in Tokugawa Days, 1603-1868* (New York, 1968), 110-114, 118.

9. 蘇同炳,《台灣今古談》(臺北市:臺灣商務印書館, 1986), 頁 74; *see also* 施琅,〈恭陳臺灣棄留疏〉, *in*《靖海紀事》(臺北市:臺灣銀行經濟研究室, 1957-61), 卷下, 頁 62-63。

10. 李光地,《榕村全集》, *quoted in* 陳捷先,〈康熙與台灣開發〉, *in*《歷史月刊》(2000 年 10 月), 頁 51。

11. 魏源,《聖武記》(台北市:中華, 1962), 卷 8。

12. 劉良璧,《重修福建臺灣府志》(臺北市:臺灣銀行經濟研究室, 1961), 卷 1, 頁 37, 卷 2, 頁 39; *see also* 史明,《台灣人四百年史》(臺北市:草根文化出版社, 1998), 頁 121。

13. 清世宗敕編,《聖祖仁皇帝聖訓》, 卷 2。

14. 清世宗敕編,《聖祖仁皇帝庭訊格言》, 卷 64; *see also* Jonathan D. Spence, *Emperor of China* (Vintage Books, 1988), 35.

15. 清世宗敕編,《聖祖仁皇帝庭訊格言》, 卷 64; *see also* Jonathan D. Spence, *Emperor of China* (Vintage Books, 1988), p. 35.

16. 清世宗敕編,《聖祖仁皇帝聖訓》, 卷 50,《台灣編歸版圖之上論》; *see also* 史明,《台灣人四百年史》(草根文化出版社, 1998), 頁 122。

17. For a full analysis of Shi Lang and why the Qing occupied Taiwan *see* Macabe Keliher,〈施琅的故事—清朝爲何佔領台灣〉《台灣文獻》卷 53 期 4, 2002.12.31)。

18. 李光地,《榕村全集》(臺北市:文友, 1972), 卷 11。

19. *Quoted in* 陳捷先，〈從清代檔案看雍正治台〉，*in*《故宮學術季刊》（台北，2001.6.16），頁 1。

20. *See* 蔡相煇，〈明清政權更迭與臺灣民間信仰關係之研究〉（文化大學博士論文，1984），頁 65；周雪玉，《施琅攻台的功與過》（臺北市：臺原出版社，1988），頁 139。

21. 周鍾瑄，《諸羅縣志》，（臺北市：臺灣銀行經濟研究室，1962），卷 6〈賦役志〉，頁 87。*See also* John Robert Shepherd, *Statecraft and Political Economy on the Taiwan Frontier: 1600-1800* (Stanford, 1993), 229.

22. 陳秋坤，〈清代中葉台灣農村經濟危機與業佃糾紛──以岸裡社潘姓業主的天業經營為中心〉，1760-1850, in《國家科學委員會研究彙刊》人文及社會科學，1994 年 7 月，卷 4 期 2，頁 151-172。

23.《雍正硃批奏摺選輯》（臺北市：臺灣銀行經濟研究室，1972），頁 113-114。*See also* John Robert Shepherd, *Statecraft and Political Economy on the Taiwan Frontier: 1600-1800* (Stanford, 1993), 233-234.

24. *See* John Robert Shepherd, *Statecraft and Political Economy on the Taiwan Frontier: 1600-1800* (Stanford, 1993), 229.

25. *Quoted in* Mark A. Allee, *Law and Local Society in Late Imperial China, Northern Taiwan in the Nineteenth Century* (Stanford, 1994), 65.

26. *Quoted in* M. Paske-Smith, *Western Barbarians in Japan and Formosa in Tokugawa Days*, 1603-1868 (New York, 1968), 118.

27. 范咸，《重修臺灣府志》（臺北市：臺灣銀行經濟研究室，1961），卷 5〈賦役〉，頁 211。

28. 季麒光，〈再陳台灣事宜文〉*in*《臺灣縣志》（臺北市：臺灣銀行經濟研究室，1957-61），藝文志 10，頁 232。

29. 郁永河，《裨海紀遊》（臺北市：臺灣銀行經濟研究室，1957-61），卷下，頁 30。

30. 郁永河，《裨海紀遊》（臺北市：臺灣銀行經濟研究室，1957-61），卷下，頁 29。

31. Fr. Jacinto Esquivel, 1632, *in* Jose Eugenio Borao Mateo, ed., *Spaniards in Taiwan Vol. I: 1582-1641*, (Taipei, 2001), 174.

32. 郁永河，《裨海紀遊》（臺北市：臺灣銀行經濟研究室，1957-61），卷中，頁 27。

PART 4 (pp. 82-101)

QUOTE 1: 郁永河，《裨海紀遊》（臺北市：臺灣銀行經濟研究室，1957-61），卷中，頁 32。

QUOTE 2: Missive, Commander Gerrit Fredericksz de Witt to Goveror-General Pieter de Carpentier, Tayouan, November 15, 1626, VOC 1090, fol. 196-206, in, Leonard Blusse, Natalie Everts and Evelien Frech, ed., *The Formosan*

Encounter: Notes on Formosa's Aboriginal Society: A Selection of Documents from Dutch Archival Sources, Vol. I: 1623-1635 (Taipei, 1999), 52.

1. VOC 1081, fol. 105-109, *in* Leonard Blusse, Natalie Everts and Evelien Frech, ed., *The Formosan Encounter: Notes on Formosa's Aboriginal Society: A Selection of Documents from Dutch Archival Sources, Vol I: 1623-1635* (Taipei, 1999), 15.

2. Reverend Georgius Candidius, Sincan, 27 December 1628, *in* Leonard Blusse, Natalie Everts and Evelien Frech, ed., *The Formosan Encounter: Notes on Formosa's Aboriginal Society: A Selection of Documents from Dutch Archival Sources, Vol. I: 1623-1635* (Taipei, 1999), 125.

3. *Quoted in* Leonard Blusse, 'Another Voice from the Past: the Dutch occupation of Peng-hu and the first Dutch settlement on Taiwan, between Myth and Reality' (paper presented at *The International Symposium on the Image of Taiwan During the Dutch Period*, Oct. 14, 2001), 58.

4. *Quoted in* Leonard Blusse, 'Another Voice from the Past: the Dutch occupation of Peng-hu and the first Dutch settlement on Taiwan, between Myth and Reality' (paper presented at *The International Symposium on the Image of Taiwan During the Dutch Period*, Oct. 14, 2001), 58.

5. Message, Governor Martinus Sonck, Tayouan, 9 April 1625, DRB, p.144-146, *in* Leonard Blusse, Natalie Everts and Evelien Frech, ed., *The Formosan Encounter: Notes on Formosa's Aboriginal Society: A Selection of Documents from Dutch Archival Sources, Vol. I: 1623-1635* (Taipei, 1999), 42.

6. Missive, Commander Gerrit Fredericksz de Witt to Goveror-General Pieter de Carpentier, Tayouan, November 15, 1626, VOC 1090, fol. 196-206, *in* Leonard Blusse, Natalie Everts and Evelien Frech, ed., *The Formosan Encounter: Notes on Formosa's Aboriginal Society: A Selection of Documents from Dutch Archival Sources, Vol. I: 1623-1635* (Taipei, 1999), 52.

7. Discourse by the Reverend Georgius Candidius, Sincan, 27 December 1628, Rijksarchief Utrecht, Family Archive Huydecoper, R.67, No. 621, *in* Leonard Blusse, Natalie Everts and Evelien Frech, ed., *The Formosan Encounter: Notes on Formosa's Aboriginal Society: A Selection of Documents from Dutch Archival Sources, Vol. I: 1623-1635* (Taipei, 1999), 117, 120.

8. Commander Claes Bruyu, November 1633, VOC 5051, *in* Leonard Blusse and Natalie Everts, ed., *The Formosan Encounter: Notes on Formosa's Aboriginal Society: A Selection of Documents from Dutch Archival Sources, Vol. II: 1636-1645* (Taipei, 2000), 6-7.

9. General Missive, 3 February 1626, VOC 1086, fol. 5, *in* Leonard Blusse, Natalie Everts and Evelien Frech, ed., *The Formosan Encounter: Notes on Formosa's Aboriginal Society: A Selection of Documents from Dutch Archival Sources, Vol. I: 1623-1635* (Taipei, 1999), 47.

10. Missive, Commander Gerrit Fredericksz de Witt to Governor-General Pieter de Carpentier, Tayouan, 29 October 1625, VOC 1087, fol. 385-396, *in* Leonard Blusse, Natalie Everts and Evelien Frech, ed., *The Formosan Encounter: Notes on Formosa's Aboriginal Society: A Selection of Documents from Dutch Archival Sources, Vol I: 1623-1635* (Taipei, 1999), 44-45

11. *See* Governor Hans Putmans to the Amsterdam Chamber, Tayouan, 15 September 1629, VOC 1098, fol. 33-38; Dagregister Zeelandia, 28 November 1629, VOC 1101, fol. 390, DRZ, Vol. 1, p. 5, *in* Leonard Blusse, Natalie Everts and Evelien Frech, ed., *The Formosan Encounter: Notes on Formosa's Aboriginal Society: A Selection of Documents from Dutch Archival Sources, Vol. I: 1623-1635* (Taipei, 1999), 157, 166.

12. 郁永河,《裨海紀遊》(臺北市：臺灣銀行經濟研究室, 1957-61), 卷下, 頁 36。

13. *See* Leonard Blusse, Natalie Everts and Evelien Frech, ed., *The Formosan Encounter: Notes on Formosa's Aboriginal Society: A Selection of Documents from Dutch Archival Sources, Vol. I: 1623-1635* (Taipei, 1999), 53, 123.

14. Missive Reverend Georgius Candidius to Governor-General Jan Pietersz. Coen. Sincan, 20 August 1628, VOC 1096, fol. 199-202, *in* Leonard Blusse, Natalie Everts and Evelien Frech, ed., *The Formosan Encounter: Notes on Formosa's Aboriginal Society: A Selection of Documents from Dutch Archival Sources, Vol. I: 1623-1635* (Taipei, 1999), 87.

15. Missive, Governor Martinus Sonck to Governor-General Pieter de Carpentier, Tayouan, 12 December 1624, VOC 1083, fol. 49-54, *in* Leonard Blusse, Natalie Everts and Evelien Frech, ed., *The Formosan Encounter: Notes on Formosa's Aboriginal Society: A Selection of Documents from Dutch Archival Sources, Vol. I: 1623-1635* (Taipei, 1999), 36.

16. 郁永河,《裨海紀遊》(臺北市：臺灣銀行經濟研究室, 1957-61), 卷下, 頁 36。

17. Missive, Reverend Robertus Junius to Governor Hans Putmans, Sincan, 25 November 1633, in, Leonard Blusse, Natalie Everts and Evelien Frech, ed., *The Formosan Encounter: Notes on Formosa's Aboriginal Society: A Selection of Documents from Dutch Archival Sources, Vol. I: 1623-1635* (Taipei, 1999), 224.

18. Missive, Governor Hans Putmans to the Amsterdam Chamber, Tayouan, 23 October 1635, VOC 1111, fol. 257-260, *in* Leonard Blusse, Natalie Everts and Evelien Frech, ed., *The Formosan Encounter: Notes on Formosa's Aboriginal Society: A Selection of Documents from Dutch Archival Sources, Vol. I: 1623-1635* (Taipei, 1999), 291.

19. Missive, Governor Hans Putmans to Governor-General Hendrick Brouwer, Tayouan, 18 January 1636, VOC 1120, fol. 219-224, *in* Leonard Blusse, Natalie Everts and Evelien Frech, ed., *The Formosan Encounter: Notes on Formosa's Aboriginal Society: A Selection of Documents from Dutch Archival Sources, Vol. I: 1623-1635* (Taipei, 1999), 11, 13.

20. 高拱乾, 《臺灣府志》(台北市 : 臺灣銀行經濟研究室, 1960), 卷 7 〈風土志〉, 頁187。

21. Discourse by the Reverend Georgius Candidius, Sincan, 27 December 1628, Rijksarchief Utrecht, Family Archive Huydecoper, R.67, No. 621, *in* Leonard Blusse, Natalie Everts and Evelien Frech, ed., *The Formosan Encounter: Notes on Formosa's Aboriginal Society: A Selection of Documents from Dutch Archival Sources, Vol. I: 1623-1635* (Taipei, 1999), 112.

22. In, Leonard Blusse, 'Another Voice from the Past: the Dutch occupation of Peng-hu and the first Dutch settlement on Taiwan, between Myth and Reality' (paper presented at, *The International Symposium on the Image of Taiwan During the Dutch Period*, Oct. 14, 2001), 57.

23. In, Leonard Blusse, 'Another Voice from the Past: the Dutch occupation of Peng-hu and the first Dutch settlement on Taiwan, between Myth and Reality' (paper presented at *The International Symposium on the Image of Taiwan During the Dutch Period*, Oct. 14, 2001), 59.

24. Message, Governor Marinus Sonck, Tayouan, 9 April 1625, DRB, 144-146, in, Leonard Blusse, Natalie Everts and Evelien Frech, ed., *The Formosan Encounter: Notes on Formosa's Aboriginal Society: A Selection of Documents from Dutch Archival Sources, Vol. I: 1623-1635* (Taipei, 1999), 41.

25. P. de Carpentier, 13 December 1626, VOC 1090, *in* 程紹剛, 《荷蘭人在福爾摩莎》(臺北市 : 聯經, 2000), 頁 60。

26. Figures from, 楊彥杰, 《荷據時代台灣史》(臺北市 : 聯經, 2000), 頁 170。

27. *See* Hsu Wen-hsiung, 'Aboriginal Island to Chinese Frontier: The Development of Taiwan before 1683', *in* Ronald G. Knapp, ed., *China's Island Frontier: Studies in the Historical Geography of Taiwan*, (Hawaii, 1980), 17.

28. 夏琳，《閩海紀要》（臺北市：臺灣銀行經濟研究室, 1958），卷上，頁 27。

29. 江日昇，《臺灣外記》（臺北市：臺灣銀行經濟研究室, 1957-61），卷 6，頁 236。

30. 高拱乾，《臺灣府志》（台北市：臺灣銀行經濟研究室, 1960），卷 7〈風土志〉，頁 186。

PART 5 (pp. 102-117)

QUOTE: 郁永河，《裨海紀遊》（臺北市：臺灣銀行經濟研究室, 1957-61），卷中，頁 20。

1. 郁永河，《裨海紀遊》（臺北市：臺灣銀行經濟研究室, 1957-61），卷上，頁 13。

2. W.A. Pickering, *Pioneering in Formosa* (London, 1898) 37,99.

3. 周璽等纂，《彰化縣誌》（臺北市：臺灣銀行發行, 1957），卷 9〈風俗志〉。

4. *See* John Robert Shepherd, *Statecraft and Political Economy on the Taiwan Frontier: 1600-1800* (Stanford, 1993), 216-222.

5. *See* John Robert Shepherd, *Statecraft and Political Economy on the Taiwan Frontier: 1600-1800* (Stanford, 1993), 113.

6. 陳璸，〈條陳經理海疆北路事宜〉，*in*《陳清端公文選》（臺北市：臺灣銀行經濟研究室, 1961），頁 15。

7. 郁永河，《裨海紀遊》（臺北市：臺灣銀行經濟研究室, 1957-61），卷下，頁 37-38。

8. 陳璸，〈條陳經理海疆北路事宜〉，*in*《陳清端公文選》（臺北市：臺灣銀行經濟研究室, 1961），頁 15。

9. 黃叔璥，《臺海使槎錄》（臺北市：臺灣銀行經濟研究室, 1957），卷 8〈番俗雜記，166; *see also*, John Robert Shepherd, *Statecraft and Political Economy on the Taiwan Frontier: 1600-1800* (Stanford, 1993), 224.

10. 陳璸，〈條陳經理海疆北路事宜〉，*in*《陳清端公文選》（臺北市：臺灣銀行經濟研究室, 1961），頁 15。

11. WM. Campbell, *Formosa Under the Dutch* (London, 1903), 510.

12. 《雍正朝漢文硃批奏摺匯編》，官中檔雍正朝奏摺（上海：江蘇古籍出版社, 1989-1991）*see also* John Robert Shepherd, *Statecraft and Political Economy on the Taiwan Frontier: 1600-1800* (Stanford, 1993), 128.

13. 陳璸，〈條陳經理海疆北路事宜〉, *in*《陳清端公文選》（臺北市：臺灣銀行經濟研究室, 1961），頁 15.

14. *Quoted in* Mark A. Allee, *Law and Local Society in Late Imperial China, Northern Taiwan in the Nineteenth Century* (Stanford, 1994), 123.

PART 6 (pp. 118-127)

QUOTE: *La Terre Illustree* (Paris, 1890-1891).

1. Descriptions from, 黃叔璥, 〈番俗六考〉, *in*《臺海使槎錄》(臺北市：臺灣銀行經濟研究室, 1957), 卷 6, 頁 133; 郁永河, 《裨海紀遊》(臺北市：臺灣銀行經濟研究室, 1957-61), 卷中, 頁 22.

2. *See* 周元文, 《重修臺灣府志》(臺北市：臺灣銀行經濟研究室, 1960), 卷 7 〈風土志〉, 頁 240; 郁永河, 《裨海紀遊》(臺北市：臺灣銀行經濟研究室, 1957-61), 卷上, 頁 13。

3. 范咸, 《重修臺灣府志》(臺北市：臺灣銀行經濟研究室, 1961), 卷 15, 頁 451; 連橫, 《雅堂文集》(臺北市：臺灣銀行經濟研究室, 1964), 卷 3, 頁 178。

PART 7 (pp. 128-141)

QUOTE: 郁永河, 《裨海紀遊》(臺北市：臺灣銀行經濟研究室, 1957-61), 卷中。

1. *Quoted in* Leonard Blusse and Natalie Everts, ed., *The Formosan Encounter: Notes on Formosa's Aboriginal Society: A Selection of Documents from Dutch Archival Sources, Vol. II: 1636-1645* (Taipei, 2000), 455.

2. 郁永河, 《裨海紀遊》(臺北市：臺灣銀行經濟研究室, 1957-61), 卷下, 頁 36。

3. 黃叔璥, 〈番俗六考〉, *in*《臺海使槎錄》(臺北市：臺灣銀行經濟研究室, 1957), 卷 6, 頁 128。

4. 連雅堂, 《臺灣通史》(臺北市：臺灣銀行經濟研究室, 1957-61), 卷 15 〈扶墾志〉, 頁 417。

5. 劉良璧, 《重修福建臺灣府志》(臺北市：臺灣銀行經濟研究室, 1961), 卷 20, 598; *see also* 陸傳傑, 《裨海紀遊新注》(臺北市：大地地理, 2001), 頁 55。

6. 郁永河, 《裨海紀遊》(臺北市：臺灣銀行經濟研究室, 1957-61), 卷下, 頁 36。

7. 郁永河, 〈番境補遺〉, *in*《裨海紀遊》(臺北市：臺灣銀行經濟研究室, 1957-61), 頁 57; 唐贊袞, 《臺陽見聞錄》(臺北市：臺灣銀行經濟研究室, 1957-61), 卷下, 頁 177。

8. 郁永河, 〈番境補遺〉, *in*《裨海紀遊》(臺北市：臺灣銀行經濟研究室, 1957-61), 頁 57。

9. Juan Cerezo de Salamanca to the King, August 10, 1634 *in* Jose Eugenio Borao Mateo, ed., *Spaniards in Taiwan Vol. I: 1582-1641* (Taipei, 2001), 218.

10. Governor Juan Nino de Tavora to His Majesty, the King, August 1, 1629, document 50, *in* Jose Eugenio Borao Mateo, ed., *Spaniards in Taiwan Vol. I: 1582-1641* (Taipei, 2001), 138.

11. January 22, 1637, *in* Jose Eugenio Borao Mateo, ed., *Spaniards in Taiwan Vol. I: 1582-1641* (Taipei, 2001), 262.

12. *See* Jose Eugenio Borao Mateo, ed., *Spaniards in Taiwan Vol. I: 1582-1641* (Taipei, 2001), 175, 195, 199-203.

13. Fr. Jancinto Esquivel, 1632, *in* Jose Eugenio Borao Mateo, ed., *Spaniards in Taiwan Vol. I: 1582-1641* (Taipei, 2001), 181.

14. Act of the council, January 22, 1637, *in* Jose Eugenio Borao Mateo, ed., *Spaniards in Taiwan Vol. I: 1582-1641* (Taipei, 2001), 264.

15. Fr. Jancinto Esquivel, 1632, *in* Jose Eugenio Borao Mateo, ed., *Spaniards in Taiwan Vol. I: 1582-1641* (Taipei, 2001), 179-181.

16. Diego Aduarte, 1640, *in* Jose Eugenio Borao Mateo, ed., *Spaniards in Taiwan Vol. I: 1582-1641* (Taipei, 2001), 244.

17. VOC 1120, May 21, 1636, *in* Jose Eugenio Borao Mateo, ed, *Spaniards in Taiwan Vol. I: 1582-1641.* (Taipei, 2001), 249.

18. Sebastian Hurtado de Corcurera to the King, *in* Jose Eugenio Borao Mateo, ed., *Spaniards in Taiwan Vol. I: 1582-1641* (Taipei, 2001), 275.

19. Act of the council, January 22, 1637, *in* Jose Eugenio Borao Mateo, ed., *Spaniards in Taiwan Vol. I: 1582-1641* (Taipei, 2001), 266.

20. Juan Cevicos, December 20, 1627, *in* Jose Eugenio Borao Mateo, ed., *Spaniards in Taiwan Vol. I: 1582-1641* (Taipei, 2001), 109-110.

21. Juan Cerezo de Salamanca to the King, August 10, 1634, *in* Jose Eugenio Borao Mateo, ed., *Spaniards in Taiwan Vol. I: 1582-1641* (Taipei, 2001), 218.

22. Gonzalo Prtillo, Governor of Isla Hermosa, October 11, 1641, *in* Jose Eugenio Borao Mateo, ed., *Spaniards in Taiwan Vol. I: 1582-1641* (Taipei, 2001), 332-333.

23. Captain Harouse, August 28, 1642, *in* Jose Eugenio Borao Mateo, ed., *Spaniards in Taiwan Vol. II: 1642-2682* (Taipei, 2002), 379.

24. Fr. Juan de los Angeles, March 1643, *in* Jose Eugenio Borao Mateo, ed., *Spaniards in Taiwan Vol. II: 1642-1682* (Taipei, 2002), 414.

25. *See* WM. Campbell, *Formosa Under the Dutch* (London, 1903), 496.

26. *See* WM. Campbell, *Formosa Under the Dutch* (London, 1903), 62.

PART 8 (pp. 142-159)

QUOTE 1: 《眞元妙道要略》, *quoted in* 趙鐵寒, 《火藥的發明》 (國立編譯館, 1978), 頁 19。

QUOTE 2: *Quoted in* Joseph Needham, *Gunpowder as the 4th Power* (Hong Kong, 1985), 2.

1. *See* 翁佳音,《大台北古地圖考釋》(台北縣立文化中心, 1998), 頁 40-46。

2. *Quoted in* Leonard Blusse, *Another Voice from the Past: the Dutch occupation of Peng-hu and the first Dutch settlement on Taiwan, between Myth and Reality* (paper presented at *The International Symposium on the Image of Taiwan During the Dutch Period*, Oct. 14, 2001) 57-8.

3. Reverend Georgius Candidius, Sincan, 27 December 1628, *in* Leonard Blusse, Natalie Everts and Evelien Frech, ed., *The Formosan Encounter: Notes on Formosa's Aboriginal Society: A Selection of Documents from Dutch Archival Sources, Vol. I: 1623-1635* (Taipei, 1999), 113.

4. 郁永河,《裨海紀遊》(臺北市:臺灣銀行經濟研究室, 1957-61), 卷下, 頁 38。

5. 郁永河,《裨海紀遊》(臺北市:臺灣銀行經濟研究室, 1957-61), 卷下, 頁 37。

6. *Quoted in* Ian McMorran, 'Wang Fu-Chih and the Yung-li Court', *Jonathan D. Spence and John E. Wills Jr., ed.* in From Ming to Ching: conquest, region, and continuity in 17th century China, (Yale, 1979), 157.

7. 郁永河,《裨海紀遊》(臺北市:臺灣銀行經濟研究室, 1957-61), 卷下, 頁 31。

8. 清世宗敕編,《聖祖仁皇帝聖訓》, 卷 2。

9. 郁永河,《裨海紀遊》(臺北市:臺灣銀行經濟研究室, 1957-61), 卷下, 31。

10. 盧之頤,《本草乘雅半偈》, 清順治丁亥(四年)錢塘盧氏月樞閣刊本(台北市: 國立中央圖書館縮影室, 1981), 卷 6, 四庫全書子部 85; *Quoted in* 吳奇娜,《17-19 世紀台灣硫磺貿易之政策轉變研究》(國立成功大學碩士論文, 2000 年), 頁 19。

11. 〈眞元妙道要略〉, *quoted in* 趙鐵寒,《火藥的發明》(國立編譯館, 1978), 19 頁; *see also* Joseph Needham, *Science and Civilisation in China Vol. 5-7* (Cambridge, 1986), 112.

12. *Quoted in* Joseph Needham, *Science and Civilisation in China, Vol. 5-7* (Cambridge, 1986), 117.

13. *Quotes from*, Joseph Needham, *Science and Civilisation in China Vol. 5-7* (Cambridge, 1986), 97, 111.

14. *Quoted in* Joseph Needham, *Science and Civilisation in China Vol. 5-7* (Cambridge, 1986), xxx.

15. The first reference to *huo yao* appeared in the 1040 AD text《武經總要》。

16. *See* 馮家昇,《火藥的發明和西傳》(上海人民出版社, 1962), 頁 75。

17. *Quoted in* Joseph Needham, *Science and Civilisation in China Vol. 5-7* (Cambridge, 1986), 48.

18. *Quoted in* Joseph Needham, *Gunpowder as the 4th Power* (Hong Kong, 1985), 2.

PART 9, pages 160-171

QUOTE 郁永河，《裨海紀遊》（臺北市：臺灣銀行經濟研究室，1957-61），頁 26。

1. *See* 黃榮洛，〈勸君切某過台灣──「渡台悲歌」的發現研究〉，*in*《渡臺悲歌：台灣的開拓與抗爭史話》（台北市：臺原出版社，1989），頁 24。

2. January 22, 1637, *in Spaniards in Taiwan Vol. I: 1582-1641*, Jose Eugenio Borao Mateo, ed. (Taipei, 2001), 263.

3. W.A. Pickering, *Pioneering in Formosa* (London, 1898), 93.

4. George L. Mackay, *From Far Formosa: The Island its People and Missions* (New York, 1896), 42.

5. 郁永河，〈番境補遺〉，*in*《裨海紀遊》（臺北市：臺灣銀行經濟研究室，1957-61），頁 27。

6. Reverend W. Campbell, *Sketches From Formosa* (London & New York, 1915), 122.

7. Reverend W. Campbell, *Sketches From Formosa* (London & New York, 1915), 120.

PART 10 (pp. 172-183)

QUOTE: 郁永河，《裨海紀遊》（臺北市：臺灣銀行經濟研究室，1957-61），卷上，頁 13。

1. 郁永河，《裨海紀遊》（臺北市：臺灣銀行經濟研究室，1957-61），卷上，頁 13。

2. 高拱乾，《臺灣府志》（臺北市：臺灣銀行經濟研究室，1960），卷 7〈風土志〉，頁 194。

3. 王必昌，《重修臺灣縣志》（臺北市：臺灣銀行經濟研究室，1961），卷 2〈山水志〉，頁 76；*see also* 朱瑪瓏，《近代颱風知識的轉變》（台大歷史碩士，2000 年），頁 31。

4. 〈條陳澎湖善後事宜〉，*quoted in* 朱瑪瓏，《近代颱風知識的轉變》（台大歷史碩士，2000 年），頁 31。

5. 高拱乾，《臺灣府志》（臺北市：臺灣銀行經濟研究室，1960），卷 7〈風土志〉，頁 194。

PART11 (pp. 184-197)

QUOTE: 郁永河，《裨海紀遊》（臺北市：臺灣銀行經濟研究室，1957-61），卷下，頁 42。

1. *Quoted in* C.R. Boxer, *The Christian Century in Japan: 1549-1650* (Berkley, 1951), 126, 127.

2. See, 連雅堂，《臺灣通史》（臺北市：臺銀經研室，1957-61），卷 1〈開闢紀〉，24.3。

3. 陳第，〈東番記〉（沈有容，《閩海贈言》，臺北市：臺灣銀行經濟研究室 1959）。

4. *See,* 翁佳音，《臺灣，福佬的海洋地名》（未出版），頁 4。

5. Adam Verhult, 26 March-26 April 1623, in the journal of Cornelis Reyersen. VOC 1081, fol. 65-67, *in* Leonard Blusse, Natalie Everts and Evelien Frech, ed., *The Formosan Encounter: Notes on Formosa's Aboriginal Society: A Selection of Documents from Dutch Archival Sources, Vol. I: 1623-1635* (Taipei, 1999), 2.

6. *See*《蓉洲文稿》。

7. 郁永河，《裨海紀遊》，卷下，頁 29。

ACKNOWLEDGEMENTS

I n a book on a topic for which not only the answers remain hidden, but the fundamental questions are still being asked, one undoubtedly receives a great deal of help from those asking and discovering. Professor Lai Fu-shun of the Chinese Cultural University spent countless hours with me discussing Chinese history and the first discovery of Taiwan. He provided me with invaluable documents from primary Qing source records, and was always ready to answer my late night inquires on Chinese and Taiwanese history. He also read through the manuscript in its early form correcting many would-be-embarrassing errors. Likewise, Ang Kaim at the Institute of Taiwan History, Academia Sinica, unconditionally lent me his time and his papers in progress. His careful reading of the manuscript provided invaluable nitpicking over place names and geological facts; he also set my dates straight. Professor Chen Hsin-hsiung of Cheng Kung University commented on an early version of the manuscript as did Chen Chiu-kun and Chen Kuo-tung at the Academia Sinica. Throughout the research process I pestered all of them enough to wear out my welcome, their patience for which I am grateful. Professor Tu Cheng-sheng also provided many comments on the text as he prepared a wonderful explanatory preface.

I am fortunate as well to have friends and colleagues who take an interest the subject of Taiwan history and what I have tried to do with it. Julian Baum has encouraged the project from its birth over a bowl of noodles on the back streets of Taipei, to making the final copyedit on the manuscript. His time and effort in helping rushing the book to completion has been more than any good friend could demand. Iris Tam has read through and corrected numerous versions. Lambert van der Aalsvoort gave a careful read through the entire manuscript and made many important suggestions, and Peter Christopher's editorial comments brought to my attention discrepancies in the narrative. Rick Balkan's suggestions helped develop the book's prologue, and my father, George Keliher, corrected my sailing terminology. Zoe Keliher and Nina Steffens made me rethink my treatment of Yu. Dr. Lin Tien-ho's moral support in the cool waters of the swimming pool every morning, inquiring on my progress, pushed me onwards. He unconditionally lent me his library card, paid my overdue fines, and at times even brought the books I needed to my front door, giving me access to volumes I would have had a real headache digging up elsewhere.

The final version of the text could not have arrived without the help of Julian Baum, Jim Boyce, Jason Dean, and Matthew Smith. Nor would it be worthy of the public's eyes without the expert copyediting of Heidi Steffens. Their suggestions have aligned a crooked structure and cleaned up garbled sentences. Alicia Beebe took over the book's design at the last minute, her time and expertise I am eternally grateful for.

My assistant Yen Jvnyi had an essential role in this project. Her research capabilities made sure I had every secondary source on the subject matter, not to mention the essential primary documents, and her insights into the territory have kept me from running astray more than once. This book would not be half of what it is without her.

杜　序

杜正勝，國立故宮博物院院長

郁永河這個人，在中國知識份子傳統中是罕見的奇人，他的《裨海紀遊》是有趣的奇書，而克禮先生這本譯述，我認為可以幫助我們了解早期臺灣的歷史，所以我很樂意先讀，並且推薦給讀者共享。

關於郁永河的資料很少，只知他是浙江仁和縣（杭州附近）人，清代學者提到他，多說事蹟不可考；即使經過近代學者研究考證，也不能增加我們太多知識。不過根據他傳世最主要的著作《裨海紀遊》，我們推測他大概出生在 1650 年稍前，對中國典籍相當熟悉，吟詩作文都不差，但沒有考取功名，故亦不曾任官。他生性喜好遊歷，雖家有老母，也不辭遠遊；福建各地大概都走遍了，還到過當時被認為最蠻荒的臺灣。我們不知道他的職業，但他認識不少省縣層級的地方政府官員，推測家境不錯，應該是鄉紳型的人物。

郁永河頗有一些外洋知識，對海外國家亦有興趣，這是他不同於傳統知識份子的地方。從他的其他傳世著作，如關於明鄭的《偽鄭逸事》、臺灣原住民的《番境補遺》、中國東南海外的《海上紀略》和《宇內形勢》，都可以證明。中國傳統讀書人除當官赴任所，或犯罪被充軍，很少遠遊，有則多是五嶽名山，像郁永河親履海外之地，並且留下生動記述的人，實在絕無僅有。我說他是「奇人」，是就這個歷史脈絡說的。然而由於時代和文化傳統的限制，郁永河有他的限度。他所認識的日本、紅夷、西洋國等，含有濃厚的傳說性，遠不如當時歐洲探險、航海家對東方的了解。這是中國文化的限度，不能獨責於郁氏一人。

郁永河之所以來臺灣，是由於 1696 年福州火藥庫爆炸，受福建官員委託，第二年開春自廈門渡海經澎湖到台南登陸，然後循西部沿海北上，到達淡水、北投。他向原住民購買硫土（硫磺礦石），熬鍊成硫磺。同年冬天，從淡水返回福州。他自出發就開始寫日記，記錄沿途所見所聞，即是《裨海紀遊》。因為目的是來採硫磺，所以也稱作《採硫日記》。《裨海紀遊》是親身經歷的著作，郁永河的文筆極為生動，又能追溯歷史，所以很早就成為膾炙人口的遊記，被收在許多不同的叢書中。

郁永河到臺灣時，清朝剛統治臺灣 13 年，距離鄭成功驅逐荷蘭人有 35 年，而距離荷蘭人入侵臺灣也不過 73 年而已。因此，他在臺灣不但直接記錄當時中國統治臺灣的情狀，明鄭或荷蘭的遺留，包括制度和習俗，也可能看得到或聽得到一些。當然，當時平埔族的傳統文化保存的還相當多，他也給我們留下不少第一手資料。這本遊記基本上可以反映一些十七世紀臺灣歷史多元的面貌。

關於十七世紀臺灣的可靠文獻，荷蘭方面係以東印度公司的經營與統治為主，明鄭時代留存的直接史料甚少，清初的資料也偏於統治。郁永河雖受官方委託來台，他既不是官員，這本私人日記自然比較能傳達一個有良心的知識份子的觀點。他為平埔族所受到的壓迫極抱不平，不過他仍然無法超越傳統中國知識份子的局限，對平埔族文化並不能同情地了解。該怎樣對待所謂「不文明」民族的文化,即使是現代學者也是一個很難處理的問題,我們當然不會對郁永河期望過高。

郁永河在日記中夾雜議論,並且追溯歷史,克禮似乎師法郁永河的作法,這本 *Out of China* 也不單純只作翻譯,而是以日記為主軸,建構十七世紀臺灣的歷史。我們可以讀到鄭成功、施琅、清朝和臺灣種種相關的史事,更能讀到郁永河所不知的荷蘭和西班牙文獻。《裨海紀遊》的有趣在於探險見聞,但有些地方難免誇大。經過荷蘭、西班牙和明鄭的鎮壓和剝削,臺灣已不是一個洪荒未闢的世界,郁永河給我們營造的氣氛,傳奇成分恐怕重了一點。這方面克禮產生一些平衡的作用,他補充的史料可以使《裨海紀遊》多一些歷史成分,少一點小說的味道。

《裨海紀遊》的文字對一個西方人來說,是不容易理解的,但克禮的譯述,取捨恰當,文義掌握也很深入。尤其經過他重新組織編排,按時間為序,分別加入專題敘述,全面建構十七世紀的臺灣史,可以算是克禮的著作了。而克禮的史觀和介紹的荷、西文獻,不但豐富《裨海紀遊》的內容,對想認識自己歷史的臺灣人,或對想了解臺灣的外國人,這本 *Out of China* 都是值得一讀的。

CAST OF CHARATERS

Big Zhang 張大 : Danshui Village chief.

Candidius, Georgius: Dutch missionary.

Coyett, Fredrick: Dutch governor of Taiwan when it fell to Zheng Chenggong in 1662.

Dong Zanhou 董贊侯 : Son of Zhuluo County Magistrate. Dong accompanies Yu Yonghe to Taiwan.

Gu 顧: Yu Yonghe's travel companion from Taiwan Fu.

Junius, Robertus: Dutch missionary who arrived in Taiwan in 1628 and remained for the next fourteen years.

Kangxi 康熙 (1654-1722): Emperor of China, 1662-1722. Kangxi was responsible for deciding to occupy Taiwan.

Koxinga 國姓爺 : *see* Zheng Chenggong.

Ripon, Elie: Swiss mercenary employed by the Dutch East India Company.

Shi Lang 施琅 (1621-1696): Qing Navy Admiral. Shi Lang defeated the Zhengs on Penghu and accepted their surrender on Taiwan. He was also responsible for convincing the Qing court to annex Taiwan instead of depopulate the island and leave it to the natives.

Wang Yunsen 王雲森 : Yu Yonghe's travel companion from Fuzhou.

Wu Ying 吳英 : Qing Navy commander. Wu served under Shi Lang in the victory over the Zhengs. He was later promoted to Admiral.

Wu Zhidou 吳志斗 : A member of the thirteenth-century Chinese diplomatic delegation credited with the first landing on Taiwan in Chinese records.

Yang Xian 楊祥 : A member of the thirteenth-century century Chinese diplomatic delegation credited with the first landing on Taiwan in Chinese records.

Yu Yonghe 郁永河 *(?-?)*: Chinese literati who traveled to Taiwan in 1697 and kept a diary of his journey. This diary, published as *The Small Sea Travel Records* is one of the earliest known Chinese accounts of Taiwan.

Zheng Chenggong 鄭成功 (Koxinga) (1624-1662): Ming admiral and later a self-serving military commander. Zheng was the last of the Ming resistance against the Qing. When defeated, Zheng fled to Taiwan in 1661 and drove out the Dutch a year later. His victory was short-lived as he died within three months.

Zheng Jing 鄭經 (1642-1681): Son of Zheng Chenggong. King of Taiwan. Ruler of Dongning. Zheng Jing took over the Zheng Empire on Taiwan when his father died in 1662 until his own death in 1681. He tried to establish his kingdom's independence from China and the Qing.

Zheng Keshuang 鄭克塽 *(?-?)*: Son of Zheng Jing. Keshuang was twelve years old when his father died and he was appointed heir apparent. Within two years his government surrendered to the Qing.

LIST OF ILLUSTRATIONS

Unless noted otherwise, all illustrations are courtesy of SMC Publishing Inc.

COLOR ILLUSTRATIONS APPEARING BETWEEN PAGES 108-109

GLOSSARY OF CHINESE CHARACTERS

For the sake of consistancy, and easy conversion between languages, I have romanized all Chinese nouns according to modern mandarin pronunciation. Please note, however, that the Taiwan place names of the seventeenth century were not pronounced in mandarin but the Southern Fujian dialect (which is very similar to modern day Taiwanese) and corresponded to aborigine pronunciation. As such, "Taiwan" was pronounced "Daiwan", "Danshui" as "Tamsui", "Jilong as "Kelang", and so on.

Anping　安平

Arling Mountain　二靈山

Bali Village　八里社

Banxian Village　半線社

Bazhang Creek　八掌溪

Bietou　北投

Big Zhang　張大

Buozhou　播州

Cai Li Village　柴裡社

Cao Luyang　曹呂陽

Changzhou　常州

Chaozhou　潮州

Chen Bin　陳璸

Chen Di　陳第

Chen Yunghua　陳永華

Chikan　赤崁

Chongming Island　崇明島

Da Wan　大灣

Dadan Island　大膽島

Danshui　淡水

Daoist　道教

Dao-luo-guo Village　倒咯國社

Da-wu-jun Village　大武郡社

Dayuan　大員

Dengzhou　登州

Ding Lingwei　丁令威

Dinghai Township　定海鎮

Dong Zanhou　董贊侯

Dongning　東寧

Fang Hao　方豪

Fangkou　坊口

Fengshan　鳳山

Fujian　福建

Fuzhou　福州

Gan Hui　甘輝

Gao Qizhuo　高其倬

Gu　顧

Guandu　關渡

Guang Yu Tu　《廣輿圖》

Guangdong　廣東

Guantang Island　官塘山

Guanxi　觀喜

Gulang Yu　鼓浪嶼

Han Dynasty　漢朝

Hantou　涵頭

Hefeng Temple　和鳳宮

Heping Island　和平島

Houlong Village　後龍社

Hsinchu　新竹

Huang Liangji　黃良驥

Huang Shuqing　黃叔璥

huo yao　火藥

jia　甲

Jia-liu-wan Village　嘉溜灣社

Jia-li-xing Village　佳里興社

Jiangnan　江南

Jilong　雞籠（基隆）

Jin Dynasty　金朝

Jinmen　金門

ju　颶

Kangxi　康熙

Lan Dingyuan　藍鼎元

Li Guangdi　李光地

Li Zigu　李子鵠

Liaoluo　遼羅

Liu Guoxuan　劉國軒

Liu Zihou　柳子厚

Liuwu Dian　劉五店

Lovesick Peak　相思嶺

Lu Zhiyi　盧之頤

Lu-er-men　鹿耳門

Madou Village　麻豆社

Magong　馬公

Mai Yuan　埋冤

Mazu　媽祖

Ming Dynasty　明朝

Minjiang　閩江

Minnan　閩南

Nankan Village　南崁社

Nantai Bridge　南臺大橋

Ou Wang Village　毆王社

Penghu　澎湖

Pihai Jiyou　《裨海紀遊》

Putian　莆田

Puwei　浦尾

Puyang　莆陽

Qian Long　乾隆

Qin Shi Huang　秦始皇

Qing Dynasty　清朝

Quanzhou　泉州

Renhe Prefecture　仁和縣

Ruan Jian　阮鑒

Shalu　沙轆

Shaxi　沙溪

Shi Lang　施琅

Shuixian Temple　水仙宮

Song Dynasty　宋朝

Southern Song Dynasty　南宋朝

Tainan　臺南

Taiwan Fu　台灣府

Tingtou　亭頭

ty　颱

typhoon　颱風

Upper Bietou　內北投

Wang Fuzhi　王夫之

Wang Yunsen　王雲森

Wanli Village　宛里社

Wei River　渭水

Wei Yuan　魏源

Wu Di　武帝

Wu Ying　吳英

Wu Zhidou　吳志斗

Wuhumen　五虎門

Wulong River　烏龍江

Xi'an　西安

Xiamen　廈門

Xiandian Creek　新店溪

Xiangang Village　新港社

Xianjiang　新疆

Xiao Liuqiu　小琉球

Xinghua Jun　興化郡

Xinhua　新化

Xu Liangbin　許良彬

Yang Xian　楊祥

Yangjia Creek　楊家溪

Yangzi River　揚子江

Yishan Monastery　怡山

Yu Yonghe　郁永河

Yuan Dynasty　元朝

Yunnan　雲南

Yuxi　漁溪

Zhangzhou　漳州

Zhejiang　浙江

Zheng Chenggong　鄭成功

Zheng He　鄭和

Zheng Jing　鄭經

Zheng Keshuang　鄭克塽

Zhonggang Village　中港社

Zhou Dynasty　周朝

Zhou Xuanyu　周宣玉

Zhou Zhongxuan　周鍾瑄

Zhu Youlong　朱幼龍

Zhuluo　諸羅

Zhuqian　竹塹

INDEX

Entries are filed word-by-word. **Boldface** locators indicate extensive treatment of a topic. Locators in brackets [ ] indicate maps or illustrations; locators followed by *n* indicate footnotes.

Out of China
or Yu Yonghe's Tale of Formosa

精裝 600 元
平裝 300 元

著　　者	Macabe Keliher
發 行 人	魏　德　文
發 行 所	南天書局有限公司
地　　址	台北市羅斯福路3段283巷14弄14號
	☎(02) 2362-0190　Fax:(02) 2362-3834
郵　　撥	01080538（南天書局帳戶）
網　　址	http://www.smcbook.com.tw
電子郵件	E-mail:weitw@smcbook.com.tw
國際書號	ISBN 957-638-608-x (精裝)
	ISBN 957-638-609-8 (平裝)
版　　次	2003年3月初版一刷發行

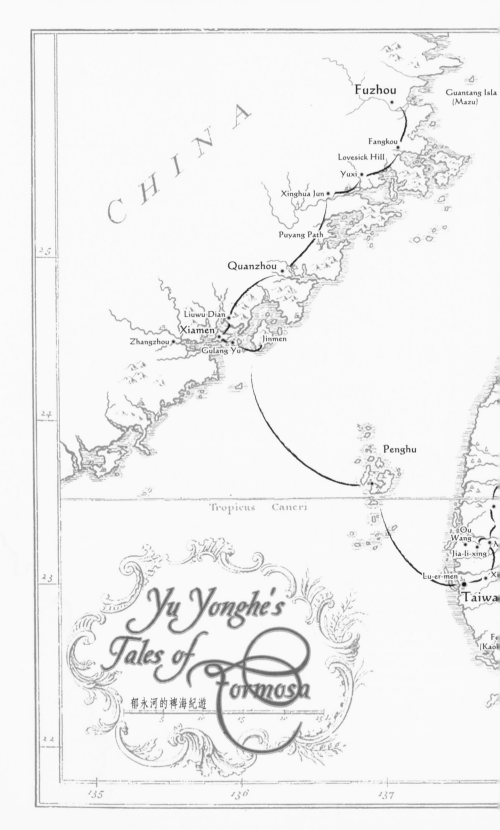

CHINA

Fuzhou

Guantang Isla
(Mazu)

Fangkou

Lovesick Hill

Yuxi

Xinghua Jun

Puyang Path

Quanzhou

Liuwu Dian

Xiamen

Zhangzhou

Gulang Yu

Jinmen

Penghu

Tropicus Cancri

Ou
Wang

Jia-li-xing

Lu-er-men

Taiwa

Fe
(Kao

Yu Yonghe's
Tales of
Formosa

郁永河的裨海紀遊

Danshui

Yu's Camp

Heping Island

Jilong

Nankan

Formosa

Zhuqian (Hsinchu)

g

an)

ISLE FORMOSE

Latitude Septentrionale:
Noorder breedte.

25

24

23

22

139

140